Enchantment of America

CALIFORNIA

By Allan Carpenter

CHILDRENS PRESS, CHICAGO

ACKNOWLEDGMENTS

For advice and assistance in the preparation of the revised edition, the author wishes to thank: Southern California Visitors Council; San Diego Convention and Visitors Bureau; Redwood Empire Association; and Department of the Army, Sacramento District, Corps of Engineers

American Airlines—Anne Vitaliano, Director of Public Relations; *Capitol Historical Society*, Washington, D. C.; *Newberry Library*, Chicago, Dr. Lawrence Towner, Director; *Northwestern University Library*, Evanston, Illinois; *United Airlines*—John P. Grember, Manager of Special Promotions; Joseph P. Hopkins, Manager, News Bureau.

UNITED STATES GOVERNMENT AGENCIES: *Department of Agriculture*—Robert Hailstock, Jr., Photography Division, Office of Communication; Donald C. Schuhart, Information Division, Soil Conservation Service. *Army*—Doran Topolosky, Public Affairs Office, Chief of Engineers, Corps of Engineers. *Department of Interior*—Louis Churchville, Director of Communications; EROS Space Program—Phillis Wiepking, Community Affairs; Charles Withington, Geologist; Mrs. Ruth Herbert, Information Specialist; Bureau of Reclamation; National Park Service—Fred Bell and the individual sites; Fish and Wildlife Service—Bob Hines, Public Affairs Office. *Library of Congress*—Dr. Alan Fern, Director of the Department of Research; Sara Wallace, Director of Publications; Dr. Walter W. Ristow, Chief, Geography and Map Division; Herbert Sandborn, Exhibits Officer. *National Archives*—Dr. James B. Rhoads, Archivist of the United States; Albert Meisel, Assistant Archivist for Educational Programs; David Eggenberger, Publications Director; Bill Leary, Still Picture Reference; James Moore, Audio-Visual Archives. *United States Postal Service*—Herb Harris, Stamps Division.

For advice, counsel, and gracious help in the first edition, the author thanks: Historical Consultant Dr. Armen Sarafian, Administrative Dean, Pasadena City College; Southern Area Consultant Richard J. Brenneman, News Bureau Director, Southern California Visitors Council; Winston Lee Sarafian; Helen Heffernan, Chief, State Bureau of Elementary Education; California State Library; Department of Fish and Game, State of California; San Diego Historical Society.

Cover photograph: Yosemite National
   Park, American Airlines
Pages 2-3: Mt. San Jacinto from Salton
   View, USDI, National Park Service,
   Joshua Tree National Monument
Page 3: (Map) USDI Geological Survey
Pages 4-5: San Francisco area, EROS Space
   Photo, USDI, Geological Survey, EROS
   Data Center

Project Editor, Revised Edition:
   Joan Downing
Assistant Editor, Revised Edition:
   Mary Reidy

Library of Congress
Cataloging in Publication Data.

Carpenter, John Allan, 1917-
   California

   (Enchantment of America)
   SUMMARY A historical and
geographical description of the state and an
account of the people who have lived there
and recent industrial and cultural developments.
   1. California—Juvenile literature.
[1. California] I. Title.
F861.3.C29   979.4   77-21101
ISBN 0-516-04105-3

Contents

A True Story to Set the Scene

COCKEYED CHARLEY

The stagecoach passengers came straggling out of the rancho station. The meal had not been good, but they had experienced much worse so far on this wild ride from San Juan Bautista.

Outside, they marveled at the strange sight of the coach's horses snorting and dashing round and round a 200-foot (about 61 meters) circle, never stopping.

Some of the passengers had found out that the horses were trained never to stop on flat ground, so at places like this station the six great horses tore around in a wide circle for half an hour while the passengers gulped their meal and the mail was sorted.

In Concord coaches weighing a ton (about .9 metric tons), the valiant travelers had thundered around the hair-raising ledges and through the pounding surf. One of them wrote, "The rest of the night was passed inside the stage, though of sleep there was not thought, such jolting and jumping over rocks and boulders; I ache all over to think of it."

They would not have been surprised if the stage had upset and thrown them into the ocean, as one had done recently at Punto Gordo. A passenger had been thrown clear over the driver's head into the surf, but was not hurt.

Often they were forced to wait for an opportunity to pass 20-ton (about 18 metric tons) wagons, pulled by forty mules. They noted how these huge cargo carriers were breaking up the improved stretches of the road faster than it could be repaired. Somehow it all has a modern sound, in spite of its setting during the 1870s.

Nor would anyone on the trip have been surprised if a masked man with a double-barreled shotgun had suddenly appeared at a strategic spot in the road to relieve them of their money. That happened much too frequently.

Wild rides of California now are at Disneyland or on the freeways.

Carpenteria was a welcome spot, for here was Shephard's Inn, run by an Iowa farmer, James Erwin Shepard. Shepard's was noted for its wonderful food, good beds, and comfortable hospitality.

There was little at that time to attract the travelers at a slow-growing shantytown called Los Angeles, although they could purchase ice cream and hot tamales there.

At last after many weary days on the trail, the travelers arrived unharmed, if they were fortunate, at the end of the line—San Diego.

But the most interesting thing about the trip was their driver. They knew he was called Charley—"One-Eyed" or "Cockeyed" Charley, because he had lost an eye when a horse kicked him.

Charley Parkhurst had been driving stages most of his life, it seemed. Like most of the stage drivers, he was proud of his skill in the extremely difficult job of a whip. Proper handling of the horses and the great coaches was an art requiring much practice, experience, and certainly courage.

Whips received high salaries for those times—$125 per month and room and board—and they deserved it.

One-eyed Charley was known as the toughest and most daring stagecoach driver in all the West. He also chewed more tobacco, swore with a greater vocabulary, and drank more than any driver in the West. The tobacco stains on his chin, his sour expression, and a black patch over his bad eye always made Charley the toughest looking person around.

Years later, when Charley died, those who had ridden his swaying coach, in fact all those who knew him or knew of his reputation, received one of the great surprises of their lives.

Tough Charley Parkhurst was a woman!

"He" had begun life as Charlotte Parkhurst of New Hampshire. "He" had been a mother and was a registered voter at Santa Cruz. "Charley" had voted in California elections almost fifty years before other women had gained the right to vote.

And so the name of Charlotte "Charley" Parkhurst lives on in the annals of the Wild West.

This is only one of the many real life stories which have made the enchantment of California live for so many people.

Lay of the Land

"This is one of the most favored spots of the earth," exclaimed the great naturalist Louis Agassiz as he first glimpsed California. When wealthy John D. Rockefeller viewed the Santa Clara Valley he called it "a picture such as I have never seen. Why! It is even worth the expense of a trip across the continent."

So many people have agreed with those famous men that California in 1963 became the most heavily populated state in the nation.

Within the boundaries of this one state are active volcanoes and silent glacier-covered peaks. There are cotton plantations and arctic meadows, covered with a carpet of Alpine flowers. There are great watery bays, shrouded with moist fog—and some of the driest stretches of the United States. Fur trappers set their lines in the bitter snow fields, while not far away desert miners toil in a superheated cloud of alkaline dust. Here is the lowest point in the United States and one of the highest, the most desolate and the most productive valleys in all the land. California is the state with its feet in the surf and its head in the clouds.

The California we know today is the result of enormous forces of nature working over millions, even billions, of years.

In a time of widespread upheaval, mountains rose out of the sea; huge areas along the continent cracked and convulsed in quakes; and volcanoes belched forth lava and ash. Great land masses rose above the ocean, to sink slowly, millions of years later, beneath the waves.

The huge central valley often fell beneath these seas. Then the rivers washed the soil from mountain slopes, piling it into the valley

Lassen Peak in Lassen Volcanic National Park.

until the valley was filled to a point above the sea. Today, the valley is covered with such a thick layer of this sediment brought down by the rivers that in many places it has been found to be 3,000-feet (about 914 meters) deep, with still no sign of bedrock.

Mightiest and most awe inspiring of all the forces that worked on California was the one which, like a mighty hand, slowly pushed a great block of granite 2 miles (about 3 kilometers) into the air. This huge chunk of rock was hundreds of miles long. We know it today as the Sierra Nevada mountain range, the largest single-block range in the United States. On top of the Sierra block as it was pushed into the sky was a much older range of mountains, called the Ancestral Sierra.

The forces that moved the Sierra toward the heavens left them with a gentle slope to the west and with one of the steepest general gradients on the North American continent on the eastern side.

Much later, huge layers of ice pushed down from the north and covered much of the land. The weight of these glaciers carved deep valleys, polished rocks or ground them into dust, and gradually melted away leaving lakes in some of the holes they had dug. Not all the ice of the glaciers has melted. Traces of this age of glaciers remain today in such places as the slopes of Mt. Shasta.

Fiery eruptions of volcanoes and the heavy blows of earthquakes have continued to change the face of California. Mt. Lassen is still considered an active volcano, and it has erupted as recently as the period between 1914 and 1917.

Today's California extends along 1,264 miles (about 2,033 kilometers) of Pacific Ocean tidal shoreline. Two main groups of small islands are all that stand between the mainland and the beaches of Hawaii. These island groups are the Santa Barbara Islands, stretching in a line off Santa Barbara and Long Beach, including famous Santa Catalina Island. The Faralone Islands, off the Golden Gate, are the second island group.

Principal features of the state are the Coast Range, the central valley, the Sierra, and to the south and east the desert regions and Imperial Valley.

Death Valley, at 282 feet (about 86 meters) below sea level, is still

The lowest point in the United States is in Death Valley.

the lowest point in the United States, but Mt. Whitney is no longer the highest mountain in the country, having lost its title when Alaska became a state.

Not many fine harbors break the California coastline, but the state does possess two of the world's finest harbors, the magnificent bays of San Francisco and San Diego.

Greatest river of California and the second largest river of the West Coast is the Sacramento. It is joined by the San Joaquin River to provide the only outlet of the central valley to the sea. Other rivers include the Klamath, Mad, Eel, Russian, Salinas, Santa Maria, Santa Ynez, Santa Clara, Pit, McCloud, Feather, Indian, Yuba, American, Fresno, Merced, Tuolumne, Stanislaus, Calaveras, Mokelumne, and Consumnes.

Some of these are dry part or most of the time, or like the Mojave River, swallowed up completely by the desert.

Most famous of California lakes is Tahoe, one of the deepest and most beautiful lakes in the country. Tahoe is shared with the neighboring state of Nevada. Lake Tahoe was formed partly by glaciers and partly by volcanoes and the movement of earth, which threw up dams of soil and rock to help make this jewel of a lake.

Largest lakes entirely within the state are Clear Lake and the Salton Sea. Among the interesting lakes of California are those in a chain of alkaline sinks, with no drainage to the sea. These include Goose, Upper Middle, and Honey. Altogether there are 8,000 lakes in California.

Footsteps on the Land

FROM LITTLE ACORNS

The smoke of a charcoal fire rose slowly into the California sky. This fire was kindled almost thirty thousand years ago. One of the earliest Californians was barbecuing an elephant.

From the remains found on Santa Rosa Island, scientists believe primitive men made California their home at least 30,000 years ago. Among these remains on Santa Rosa Island, preserved from that day to this, were the evidences of that early barbecue.

Anthropologist Louis S. B. Leakey says a site of early man in the Calico Mountains may be 75,000 years old. Others say as much as 250,000 years.

Throughout most of California, however, few remains are found of the primitive peoples who must have made their homes in the state so long ago. Before the coming of white men, native artists had created paintings on the rocks, later discovered in caves and on mountains, but who these people were or what became of them little is known.

From the mounds of shells the Indians left during the centuries, experts have determined that the Indians of California must have lived about the same for three or four thousand years before the white men found them. They had the simplest and most primitive native culture in North America.

Yet even then California had the largest population just as it does today. When the white men first came to California, more Indians lived in the central valley than in any other area of similar size anywhere on the continent.

Some of the Indian names were Maidu, Hupa, Mojave, Yuma, Achomawi, Shasta, Paiutes, and Canalino, sometimes called the "horse thief" Indians.

The Indian Village in Yosemite National Park shows how the first people in this valley lived using the plants and animals found there.

The Indians of the north and south were quite different from one another, but they all led very simple lives. The tribes did not form large groups as they did in the East. Generally, Indians of one village could not even talk with people from another village. At least twenty-one distinctly different languages were spoken, and each of these had many variations.

In the north the Indians lived in plank or sod houses. The center of their village ceremonies was the sweat house. Only chiefs and shaman, or medicine men, had any authority.

Some of the northern Indians were able to hollow trees out to make canoes. Others made woven boats like baskets. Most of the California Indians were unable to make pottery, but they were wonderfully skilled in basket weaving. They made baskets so fine and watertight they could be used for cooking food by filling them with water and dropping in red-hot stones.

Salmon were speared; other fish, clams, and mussels all added to the food supplies of the Indians, wherever such delicacies might be found. Caterpillars also were used as food.

However, in several sections of California the many oak trees provided much of the food needed by the Indians. The acorns were carefully gathered, ground into acorn meal and baked or cooked for mush. In the southeast mesquite beans were widely eaten. Piñon nuts of the Sierra slopes, ground or roasted grass seeds, berries, roots, and nuts all helped the Indians to wrest a living from the land.

One of the early explorers wrote about the Dieguenos Indians, "They did not scorn meat, but they were not basically hunters; they killed rabbits, crows, mice, snakes, frogs, coyotes, and crawfish, with weapons that varied from arrows and slings to clubs, throwing sticks, and bare hands. They were partial to grasshoppers, especially when dried, mashed, and roasted.

"They ate all sorts of insects and small animals, anything that teeth could bite, whether alive or dead, that crossed or lay in their paths. A great event for the whole region was the stranding of a dead whale; from as far as the smell carried, villages full of people came to gorge themselves and smear their bodies from head to foot with rancid blubber, to stink happily for weeks."

The Cabrillo statue, left, was a gift from Portugal. Above: The annual recreation of Cabrillo's discovery.

For their simple trading needs clam-shell disk beads were used as money. Indian wars of the brutal and fierce type so often carried on in the East were almost unknown among the Indians of California.

WHITE GODS IN GREAT CANOES

Far out on the blue sea, from time to time, the Indians of California had been told, the gods sailed by in their great canoes pushed by the white clouds strung on trees. Then one day the gods' canoe turned toward the shore, came into the great bay, and when the gods rowed in to shore in smaller canoes, the Indians watching could see that they had skin of a strange pale color, and they carried odd sticks in their hands.

The year was 1542. Leader of the white gods was the Portuguese explorer Juan Rodriguez Cabrillo, who served the Spanish King. Ever since the Spanish had come to Mexico they had heard of the wonderful lands to the north, the land of El Dorado, where great wealth in gold was found. They had heard of an easy route to the riches of China and even of a northern sea passage across America which might bring them back to Europe more easily.

17

Cabrillo had been ordered to explore this fabled land to the north. He was the first white man to sail into present-day San Diego Bay, where he anchored at Point Loma. The Indians shot arrows at the party and wounded three of them.

The expedition continued northward along the coast. Cabrillo broke either his arm or his leg; accounts of this are not clear. The broken limb did not have proper attention and he became ill. They had reached as far north as Point Reyes, when a storm forced them to turn back. They anchored at one of the Santa Barbara Islands, probably San Miguel. There Cabrillo died of the effects of his untended broken limb, and he was buried on the island in a grave unknown today. But his memory is kept alive by Cabrillo National Monument on Point Loma, overlooking the bay he first discovered, where San Diego now lies.

In spite of the death of their leader, the explorers did not pull back. Under the leadership of Bartolomé Ferrelo, they continued to the north until they were probably beyond the southern border of Oregon, and so the first expedition to reach California had sailed up and down the whole distance of the long coastline. However, they missed such important landmarks as San Francisco Bay.

Although Cabrillo's voyage was the most important, there may have been white men who actually saw present-day California before 1542. It is probable that Hernando de Alarcón, in 1540, became the first white man to view California territory when he found the mouth of the Colorado River on an exploration.

A year later, California was given its name by Francisco de Bolanos. In the same year, far to the east, the discoverer De Soto was the first to look upon the Mississippi River. Of course, the name California was applied first to the peninsula called *Lower California*, and then the name was given to the present-day state, which was known to the Spaniards as *Alta California*.

The name California was first used to describe an imaginary island in a popular Spanish novel written in 1510. The California in the novel was nearly an earthly paradise, and so the early Spaniards named the real California for their imaginary treasure island. For many years the Spaniards thought California actually was an island.

Until 1579 the Pacific was as peaceful as its name. Then the English terror of the Spaniards, Sir Francis Drake, thrust himself into the Pacific and sailed up the western shores of North America to just above San Francisco. He, too, probably failed to find the great bay just to the south of where he stopped, but he claimed the land for England in the name of Queen Elizabeth and named the area Nova Albion (or New England) because the white cliffs reminded him of Dover in England.

Not all historians believe that Drake first landed at present-day Drake's Bay, but a group of prominent men called the Drake Navigator's Guild are convinced that he did, and they have done a great deal to help prove the point.

In 1933 when some California men picked up a very old brass sheet with unknown writing on it, they tossed it aside but it was found again three years later, taken to the Bancroft Library where it may be seen. It is believed to have been the object Sir Francis Drake's chaplain described as a "Plate of brasse, fast nailed to a great and firme post" at Nova Albion. "Drake's plate" carries the words "Herr Majesty Queen Elizabeth of England and Herr Successors Forever." If this really is the work of the first English explorer of the Pacific coast, it should rank as one of the most interesting historical discoveries of modern times.

In 1854 Francisco Gali gave a more thorough examination of the California coast, but the most famous explorer after Drake was Sebastian Vizcaino. Beginning in 1602, he spent almost a year on the California coast. He renamed many places with names they still bear, including San Diego, Santa Catalina, Santa Barbara, Carmel, and Monterey Bay.

After anchoring near Point Loma on November 10, Vizcaino went ashore. On the feast day of San Diego de Alcalá he held the first Catholic services in California and named the bay in honor of the saint and his flagship which also carried the name *San Diego*.

The name Monterey has come down to us through the centuries in honor of Vizcaino's sponsor the Count of Monte Rey.

After Vizcaino's time in California, the Spaniards almost completely disregarded the area for more than one hundred fifty years.

In 1701 the Jesuit priest, Eusebio Francisco Kino, crossed the great red-colored river, the Colorado, and went into present-day California to work with the Indians, but only for a short time.

There were no white settlements in Alta California, and the Indians of the area saw little of the white men. Because the Spaniards had never brought women into the area, the Indians decided there were none and that white men must have animal mothers.

SPANIARDS ON A MISSION

Not until 1768 did the Spanish King order settlements to be made in Alta California. Acting under this order, the Visitador General of Mexico, José de Gálvez, sent expeditions both by sea and by land to make settlements at San Diego and Monterey.

The Presidio of San Diego and Mission San Diego de Alcalá were founded on July 16, 1769. On Presidio Hill, mounds of dirt were thrown up for defense, and huts were made as shelter in this first foothold of white civilization in California. Presidio Hill has sometimes been called the Plymouth Rock of the Pacific Coast. However, by this time, the settlements on the eastern coast were already almost two hundred years old.

Entrance into Monterey, *painted by Albert Bierstadt.*

Father Serra was kind to the Indians. Later Spanish overlords were not. Mural by Reverend Lawrence McLaughlin.

The man who became known as The Father of California, Father Junipero Serra, founded the first of California's twenty-one missions, at San Diego de Alcalá.

Gaspar de Portola, who might be called the first Governor of Alta California, led several difficult expeditions across the country to help develop the trail to the north from San Diego. By 1770, Portolá, Father Serra, and Father Juan Crespi established Monterey, which came to be known as the Spanish heart of California. Father Serra founded the Mission San Carlos Borromeo, June 3, 1770, at Monterey. The mission was moved to Carmel a year later. In 1775 the King of Spain named Monterey the capital of California.

In that same year the first white child was born in California on an overland expedition from Sonora to California.

Just three months before the American colonists on the Atlantic Coast were declaring their independence in 1776, the Mission San Francisco de Asis was established on San Francisco Bay.

El Pueblo de Nuestra Senora la Reina de Los Angeles de Porciuncula was founded in 1781 by Governor Don Felipe de Neve, with solemn ceremonies. As the town became larger, the long name became shorter, until today most people call it simply L.A., and the postal department calls it Los Angeles.

The number of missions in California continued to grow, and Father Serra carried on as father-president of the missions, with headquarters at Carmel, until his death in 1784.

After Father Serra's death, the missions continued to be the center of life in California. The chain of missions had grown to twenty-one. They were supposed to be spaced a comfortable day's journey apart, so that the traveler along the road from mission to mission might have a pleasant place to stop each night. This road was called El Camino Real, the King's Highway.

Last of the twenty-one missions was San Francisco Solano, established north of San Francisco Bay in 1823.

Although missions are generally thought of as being only churches, those in California were complete settlements. They included friary, church, shops, storage houses, and dormitories. Four of the missions were protected by forts called *presidios.*

To the missions came the Indian converts, who were quickly taught to work at all the tasks of the missions, tending the crops or gardens, the large herds of cattle, even becoming skilled in such jobs as tanning and working leather, blacksmithing, woodwork, and carpentry.

Unmarried Indian converts were locked up at night to keep them from temptation. Married couples lived in villages of huts outside the missions. Indians who broke the rules were severely punished. Those who escaped were hunted without letup and were brought back to be cruelly disciplined.

HIDES AND SEEK

Ships and traders of countries other than Spain were forbidden in California, but they managed to get in anyway. The first United States ship to come to California was the *Otter*, pulling into Monterey harbor from faraway Boston. Yankee, British, and other traders began to deal in the cattle hides from the great herds of the Spanish. The hides were often used in place of money and came to be known as California bank notes. Charles Dana in this famous book *Two*

Years Before the Mast, gave San Diego the humorous name "Hide Park" because of the importance of cattle-hide trading there.

Russia increased her trading activities in the California area. The Russian traders had their bases in Alaska but they decided to build a fort and headquarters in California itself in defiance of Spain's wishes.

In spite of the Spanish protest, Fort Ross was built north of Bodega Bay in 1812 by the Russians, and the Spanish could do nothing to stop them. The Russians had purchased the land for their fort from the Indians for three blankets and some tools.

Fort Ross was the most remote outpost of the Russian Empire, serving as the base for their seal and otter trade. The Russians had found that the wealthy people of China greatly prized the furs of the California sea otter. Russian trappers caught the sea otter in great numbers and shipped the furs from Fort Ross to China in exchange for the rich merchandise of the Orient. Other traders soon began to do the same thing, until the precious sea otter became almost extinct.

The Russian Czar became more and more interested in the west coast of America, and many historians feel that this was one of the important reasons President Monroe warned foreign nations to stay away from the American continents. This policy was called the Monroe Doctrine.

Another strange foreign influence came to the shores of California in 1818. Monterey was occupied for a week by the French pirate, Hippolyte de Bouchard, who had served with the patriot navy of the Republic of Buenos Aires. So in a sense it might be said that California once was occupied by Argentina, although Hippolyte was a privateer.

Not long after this, California was "occupied" by another power on a much more permanent basis.

Only about forty years after Spain had started her colonies in California, Mexico became independent from Spain and claimed California as her own. But Spain did not formally give up the rich California territory until 1825, and the Mexican flag legally flew over Monterey, the capital.

THE RANCHEROS

Under both the Spanish and Mexican rulers, large grants of land were given to important and wealthy men who became known as rancheros. There were about eight hundred important ranchos in California when the ranchero period drew to a close.

The ranch houses were built of sun-dried adobe brick. Their plain and simple lines and great comfort have made them a prominent feature of California architecture ever since. The rancho fields were worked by Indian labor, and beyond were the tremendous pasture lands where the family's vast cattle herds gazed.

It was a great day when a new land grant was formally transmitted to a ranchero, and the ancient customs are interesting. A formal survey was made. This was a neighborhood affair, a viewing of the landmarks by all who might be concerned with the boundaries of the property. Then the ranchero would pull up grass and stones from the ground and throw them to the four winds, and this was the symbol that the land now was his.

In 1831 Governor Echeandia announced his plans to secularize the missions, and some were secularized at that time. That is, they were taken out of the hands of the religious authorities. Secularization of all the missions did not occur at once.

The Indians, who were freed by Mexico, were supposed to get a portion of the mission lands. Generally they were cheated out of their shares, sold them for little or nothing, or found that they could not manage the property successfully. Many of them who tried to go back to the old simple ways of their forefathers found they had become so dependent on the rule of the missionaries that they no longer could care for themselves as the pre-white Indians in the wilderness had done. They suffered great hardships; many died.

However, it is hard to see how the Indians were in worse condition after secularizing of the missions. Father Antonio Horra said that the mission "treatment shown to the Indians is the most cruel I have ever read in history."

The period of the 1830s was a particularly confused and difficult one in California. There were so many revolutions and groups looking for power, so many claiming to be governor, and so many almost bloodless battles, and so many Indian raids, that it is difficult even to list the actual state of affairs from year to year.

During this period, José Figueroa, who was governor in 1833, has been considered the best of the Mexican governors of California.

Meanwhile, more and more outsiders were coming in. Jedediah Smith, who was called the "Bible Toter" because of the Bible he always carried, in 1826 was the first American to come overland to California. More and more Yankee trappers came in and took out fortunes in furs.

John Sutter, a Swiss, established New Helvetia in 1839, and this was the beginning of present-day Sacramento. Sutter bought out the Russian interests in California.

The first overland pioneer wagon trains left Independence, Missouri, on May 19, 1841, and arrived in the San Joaquin Valley on the fourth of November.

A strange episode occurred in 1842 when U. S. Commodore Thomas A. Catesby Jones sailed into Monterey Bay and ordered the officials to surrender. He thought mistakenly that the United States had gone to war with Mexico. When he discovered his error, he apologized and sailed away.

In 1844 the last Latin American governor, Pio Pico, gained power in a battle that took only the life of one horse, and wounded one mule. He moved his capital to Los Angeles.

In 1845, American captain John C. Frémont fortified Hawk's Peak in California and raised the American flag, but he withdrew in three days.

In 1846 the Donner party started over the mountains and were caught by an early snowstorm in what is now called Donner Pass. The exact details of this tragedy have never been known, although cannibalism has been rumored. The forty-five survivors of the original seventy-nine in the Donner party were hounded by the curiosity of others throughout life.

The growing number of American settlers in California began to encourage their government to act swiftly so that California would not fall into the hands of some other government. In June, 1846, a

The Donner Monument on U.S. Highway 40 was erected in memory of the ill-fated Donner party.

group of American squatters left Captain Frémont's camp on the Feather River and swept down on the settlement of Sonoma, which they captured along with a number of Mexican prisoners. The Americans took the petticoat of a boardinghouse keeper in Sonoma and from this snipped out a flag. On their new flag they placed cutouts—a red stripe, a star, and a grizzly bear. They claimed the region as the independent California Republic.

Because of the flag, this short-lived republic has been called the Bear Flag Republic, and the little war the Bear Flag Revolt.

At this time the Americans in California did not know that their country had been at war with Mexico for over a month.

The Bear Flag Republic lasted only twenty-three days.

26

Although he had no orders and did not know the United States was at war, Commodore John D. Sloat sailed into Monterey Harbor and raised the United States flag over the capital of California on July 7, 1846.

Several small battles marked the war in California. The bloodiest battle ever fought in the state was that of San Pasqual. Colonel Stephen Watts Kearny arrived overland with a force of about 120 men. At San Pasqual he lost a fifth of his men in a battle charge by Andres Pico, younger brother of the California governor.

The next day the Mexicans charged again and drove the Americans to a rocky hill. They were surrounded, with their supplies gone. They were forced to eat their mounts for food, and the place has been called Mule Hill ever since. The famous scout, Kit Carson, and Lieutenant Edward Beale of the Navy were able to creep through the enemy lines and get help. When 250 marines and navy men arrived, Pico withdrew.

Later, the Americans won the battle of San Gabriel. Frémont prepared to move from the north. When Andres Pico realized he was surrounded and outnumbered, he surrendered on January 13, 1847, and the war was over in California.

One of the highlights of the war had been the daring ride of John Brown, called *Juan Flaco* (Lean John). He has been named the Paul Revere of California. Lean John rode 500 miles (about 805 kilometers) from Los Angeles to San Francisco to warn every gar-

A monument to the Bear Flag Republic stands at Sonoma, north of San Francisco.

rison along the way that the Mexican leaders had recaptured the south from the Americans. The American leaders at San Francisco could hardly believe he had made the distance on horseback in only five days!

On February 2, 1848, the Treaty of Guadalupe Hidalgo, which ended the Mexican War, gave California to the United States.

CALIFORNIA IS "LODED"

Just a month before the treaty was signed, an event occurred that was to bring on one of the most exciting chapters in California's history. In January, 1848, James Wilson Marshall found a shiny metal chunk about half the size of a pea in the tailrace of Sutter's mill. Discovery of this split-pea-sized fragment caused the greatest mass movement of people since the crusades. An earlier discovery at Los Angeles in 1842 had attracted only local excitement.

Marshall and Sutter pounded the piece of metal; it spread out but did not break. It appeared to be pure gold. They tried to keep the discovery a secret, but the news leaked out.

When San Francisco learned of the gold so close by, almost every ablebodied man in the city rushed to the gold fields. Sailors and captains of boats in the harbor deserted together to seek their fortunes.

By autumn the news had spread to the Midwest, to the East, to Central America, to South America. From everywhere people started to the gold fields of California. By wagon, coach, horseback, boat, and on foot, they hastened to find their fortunes. One popular route from the East Coast was by boat to the Isthmus of Panama, overland across the isthmus, and then by boat again to California.

On some of the routes across the American prairies and deserts, the trek sometimes seemed like an endless procession. Many were not able to make such a difficult journey. One gold seeker who trudged along counted 362 abandoned wagons, the bones of 350 horses, 280 oxen, and 120 mules in one 15-mile (about 24 kilometers) stretch. Who could tell how many human graves there might be along the same length of the trail?

In less than a year, the population of San Francisco had risen from almost nothing to the incredible figure of 25,000. Fifty sailing ships per month were entering San Francisco Bay.

California's gold was no flash in the pan. The country soon learned that there was a single gold-bearing vein of quartz stretching for 150 miles (about 241 kilometers), although it was only a few miles wide. This was called the "Mother Lode."

In a single year, ten million dollars worth of gold had been taken from the middle fork of the American River. At Sonora, Big Bonanza, the richest pocket mine in the Mother Lode, yielded $160,000 worth of almost pure gold in just one day.

Two years after gold was discovered, the rush at Nevada City had brought 10,000 miners, who were working every square foot (about .09 square meters) within a 3-mile (about 4.8 kilometers) radius. In that two years, eight million dollars in gold dust and nuggets had come out of the region.

Not all the profits were made from the gold itself. Many shrewd operators realized that more could be made by selling vital supplies and setting up establishments that were essential to the miners' needs. Sausalito did a thriving business in selling its pure spring water at fifty cents per bucket to the dusty forty-niners, as they were called, across the bay. In the bars, the going rate for a drink was a pinch of gold dust, and bartenders were chosen for their large hands.

And what became of the man who started it all? "He who cried out gold," as the Mexicans called James Marshall, became a pauper. He tried to earn a poor living by selling his autograph, in a land which had not yet become the haven of autograph seekers. His landlord, John Sutter, later said that the gold rush also had ruined him. All his plans were swept away in the invasion of gold seekers.

In fact, almost all order had broken down before the push of thousands of rough and often lawless gold seekers. Even far away Los Angeles became so lawless it was called *Los Diablos*, the Devils.

The years 1848-49 were a confused period in which military law, Spanish law, and American law mingled with no law at all.

On June 3, 1849, the military governor, General Bennett Riley, issued a call for a convention to draw up a constitution for California.

Washing gold in the High Sierras

One of the great problems of the convention was deciding how much territory to include and where to draw the boundaries. Under Spain and Mexico, Alta California included not only present-day California but also Nevada, Arizona, New Mexico, Utah, and part of Colorado.

The convention decided that most of this desert area would never be worth much and that it would be difficult to govern from so far away, so they limited the boundaries to those of the present-day state.

Iowa had recently become a state. It had a modern constitution, and so the convention followed the constituion of Iowa for the most part in setting up a constitution for California.

The proposed constitution was submitted to the people of the state in the first election ever held in California under the American flag, and was adopted by the people.

California elected state officials, a legislature, and sent two senators to Washington. Governor Riley recognized the new state and resigned. For all intents and purposes California acted as a state. Nothing quite like this had ever happened before. Congress alone has the authority to create a new state, and Congress had not yet recognized California as a state. Congress criticized the irregular procedure California had followed. California was to be a free state, and those who wanted to hold on to slavery were against admitting a new free state, and a great controversy sprang up.

The two men who had been elected United State Senators from California, John C. Fremont and William M. Gwin, were not allowed to take their seats. However, after months of deadlock, Congress bowed to the will of the people of California and admitted California as the thirty-first state on September 9, 1850. The constitutional convention and the election of state officials were recognized.

Yesterday and Today

A WAR OF CRIME AND THE CRIME OF WAR

The coming of state government to California, with the first capital at San Jose, did not automatically bring law and order. In the seven years between 1849 and 1856, there were a thousand murders in San Francisco alone.

Bandits killed settlers for whatever possesions they might have, no matter how little this might be. Indians, Mexicans, blacks, and Chinese were overworked and mistreated. Many of the prosperous rancheros lost their lands because they could not prove their ownership, squatters and professionals who acted as squatters in many cases robbed them of their land.

Many of those who were mistreated felt they had no other course than to turn to banditry themselves, thus increasing the lawlessness.

The few local officials and crowded courts were powerless to do anything about the wave of crime.

And still the people crowded into California, turning the difficulties into terror. They could not find work; they could not legally take the land; there was not enough gold for all.

At last, merchants and others formed into vigilance committees, taking the law into their own hands, and lynching some of the worst of the desperadoes. Others were forced underground.

Some of the former "owners" of California, the Mexicans, became *banditi.* These were highwaymen who robbed stagecoaches of their cargo and their passengers of their valuables.

Travel on El Camino Real in those days was full of terror. The dangers of highway robbery could hardly have been exaggerated.

Butterfield's Overland Mail, Wells Fargo, and Pony Express became names still well remembered in the state. Also well remembered are the names of the famous bandits, such as Black Bart, who left cards signed the P08 (the poet), Jack Powers, and Solomon Pico.

Traveling in stagecoaches could be dangerous.

Yet in spite of all its difficulties, California was growing up. As early as 1851 the people of San Francisco were treated to regular performances of grand opera. In 1854 the capital was moved permanently to Sacramento.

News came slowly over the great distance from the national capital at Washington, D. C., to the capital of California at Sacramento, but Californians took a part in the struggle between those who wanted to do away with slavery and those who wanted to keep it.

United States Senator David Broderick, of California, who was against slavery, was killed in a duel with Davis S. Terry. Terry was a close friend of Senator William S. Gwin. Gwin and others declared that California ought to become a separate republic, where slavery would be legal. This argument split the California Democratic Party. Because of this split in 1860, Republican Abraham Lincoln was aided in winning California's vote for the Presidency by the extremely slender margin of only 1,000 votes.

In the War Between the States, California remained loyal to the Union, in spite of a plot to seize Federal strongholds in California for the South. The gold of California started east in a steady stream to play an important part in paying for the war.

With the coming of the telegraph lines across the continent in 1861, the faraway state which had been forced to wait for its news from the East, now had it almost instantly, but in spite of this, the Civil War was little felt in California.

RAILS ACROSS A CONTINENT

During the 1860s Californians were interested in events closer home. They knew that the population had reached the unbelievable figure of 379,994 in 1860. Only twenty-three years before, the entire population of California had been just 15,000.

Southern California's greatest gold rush was in 1860 when the precious metal was discovered in Holcomb Valley. At Indian Island near Eureka the white settlers were massacring the Indians. From 1862 to 1864 one of the worst droughts in California's history ruined much of the cattle business.

The Great West, *painted by Currier & Ives*

Then as the 60s drew to a close, Leland Stanford drove a golden spike that completed the first railroad across the continent, and California was never to be the same again. At last the people of the East could reach the Golden State faster, and the products of California could pass easily over the Sierras and the Rockies.

Isabella Bird, a famous English traveler described her ride over the High Sierras on the transcontinental railroad, not long after the railroad first went through.

"First came two great gaudy engines, the Grizzly Bear and the White Fox, their tenders loaded with logs, the engines with great, solitary reflecting lamps, comfortable glass houses and well-stuffed seats for the engine drivers. Next came a baggage car, a mail car, and Wells Fargo and Company's express car, loaded with bullion and valuable parcels. Then came two cars loaded with peaches and grapes; then two 'silver palace' cars; then a smoking car, at that time occupied mainly by Chinamen; and then five ordinary passenger cars, making a train about 700 feet (about 213 meters) in length.

"On a single track, sometimes carried on a narrow ledge excavated from the mountainside by men lowered from the top in baskets, overhanging ravines from 2,000 to 3,000 feet (about 609 to 914 meters) deep, the monster train snaked its way upwards, stopping sometimes in front of a few frame houses, at others where nothing was to be seen but a log cabin.

"Near the summit-pass of the Sierra, we entered the 'snow-sheds.' One of these sheds is twenty-seven miles (about 43 kilometers) long. In a few hours the mercury had fallen from 103 degrees Fahrenheit (39.4 degrees Celsius) to 29 degrees Fahrenheit (-1.7 degrees Celsius), and we had ascended 6,987 feet (about 2,130 meters) in 105 miles (about 168.9 kilometers)."

MUCH ADO

In the next few decades of California there was such a rapid-fire procession of events that it is impossible to record them all in a short history. They included the Modoc War of 1872-73, one of the last desperate attempts of the Indians to protect themselves against the overwhelming whites. A small Indian army held off fifteen times their number of white soldiers for six months. The Indian population decreased. American treatment of the Indians in California has been called shameful.

James D. Smille's painting of Golden Gate from Telegraph Hill.

The Comstock strike in Nevada brought wealth to a few Californians, but many lost their fortunes in the speculation. The state capitol was completed in 1874, and the Bank of California crashed in 1875, bringing a period of hard times.

Feeling against the Chinese laborers increased. Large numbers of Chinese had been brought in to work on the railroads and to do other heavy labor at low wages. A gang in Los Angeles wrecked the Los Angeles Chinatown and lynched nineteen Chinese.

The power of the railroads and other businesses grew, and they frequently disregarded the rights of their workers. Discontent with this situation grew. On April 1, 1878, a new constitution was ratified and proved to be a great advance in guaranteeing the rights of the people and bringing greater control of the people over their government. The Workingmen's party had a strong minority representation in the Constitutional Convention. The Constitution of 1879 is still in effect, so California has had only two constitutions.

The first big effort to promote travel for pleasure in California was in the 1880s. Thousands visited the state, attracted by the low railroad excursion fares and the claims made about the wonder of California's climate and scenic beauty.

One of the greatest of the land booms also took place in the 80s. People were persuaded to buy real estate at much more than its real worth. One promoter even stuck oranges on the spines of Joshua trees and sold the land as an orange grove. Then, of course, the boom collapsed, and many suffered.

Discovery of valuable minerals went on in California. The silver of Calico, discovered in 1881, made it one of the richest and most famous mining towns of the West. Bakersfield had a wild gold rush in 1885, and the town was destroyed by fire in 1889. Ten years later, Bakersfield became the center of another great search for minerals, in the oil rush of 1899.

In 1889, San Diego built its first flume to bring pure water to its growing population. During the ceremonies, officials praised the crystal pure qualities of the new flume water, and did not discover until several days later that the new water had been delayed and their regular well water had been substituted at the last minutes.

SHAKEUP

One of the greatest disasters of all times occurred in the beginning of the twentieth century. On April 18, 1906, a large area of California trembled violently in what has come to be known as the San Francisco earthquake. California had suffered more violent earthquakes before, but nothing to cause the damage and tragedy of this one.

Highways split with cracks 20 feet (about 6 meters) wide. Vaulted ceilings on the Stanford campus collapsed. Marble shafts in cemeteries snapped off, but in San Francisco itself the devastation was horrible.

The disintegration of buildings brought a terrible fire which raged uncontrolled for three days because all water supplies had been cut off by the quake. The entire business section, 497 blocks in the heart of the city, was destroyed. Five hundred people were killed and the damage in dollars reached 350 million.

But the fires were scarcely cold before the people of San Francisco started to rebuild.

San Diego Naval Station began in 1907. In 1908 the famous direct primary law was passed, and feelings against the Japanese people who had come to California were growing increasingly strong.

In the period of 1905 to 1911, much muckraking was carried out. This was the effort to clean up the many evils of city government in the state.

The reform movement gained strength when a reform group called the Lincoln-Roosevelt League, gained control of the California Republican Party and elected Governor Hiram Johnson in 1910. The Lincoln-Roosevelt League succeeded in pushing through twenty-two amendments to the California Constitution, including the vote for women.

Theodore Roosevelt called this "the most comprehensive programme of constructive legislation ever passed at a single session of an American legislature."

When Roosevelt split the Republican Party with his Bull Moose movement in 1912, Hiram Johnson became Roosevelt's running mate as candidate for the Vice-Presidency of the United States.

Thanks to Johnson, the Bull Moose Party carried California in 1912.

In 1913 the state called a legal holiday to observe the two hundredth anniversary of the birth of its founder, Junipero Serra.

By 1915, San Francisco had recovered so completely that it held its famous Panama Pacific International Exposition to celebrate the opening of the Panama Canal. San Diego provided its Panama-California Exposition that same year in Balboa Park in honor of the same occasion.

The year after the fair, San Diego was suffering so greatly from a drought that the famous rainmaker, Charles Hatfield was hired. He set up mysterious towers which produced explosions of vapor. The rain began within a few days but kept on so long it caused disastrous floods. Dams were washed out and people were killed. The city refused to pay Hatfield his $10,000 fee. They had asked for rain, not a flood!

California helped to make history in 1916. A dispute among the Republicans there gave the state to Woodrow Wilson by only 3,773 votes. Those votes have often been said to have changed the course of the country's history.

When World War I came in 1917, California again was far removed from the fighting, although there was the threat that the famous German Count Felix von Luckner might raid the Pacific Coast. Great numbers of Californians were then in the armed services.

After the war, a new rush to California began. In the period between 1920 and 1930, the population increased 65 percent, to a total of 5,677,251.

A view of the skyline of San Diego.

*Century City
is typical of
the modern city
of Los Angeles.*

California was one of the states most severely hit by the great depression that began in 1929. Unemployment and the problems of migrants were increased by the flood of newcomers from the dust bowls of Texas and Oklahoma. Most of those people had lost everything in the terrible drought; they had to leave their homes, and thought of California as a rich and wonderful land. They did not realize the problems the state was having.

But a few events lightened this grim period. In 1936-37 the bridges across San Francisco Bay and the Golden Gate were opened. Because of its setting and design, the Golden Gate Bridge has been considered one of the most beautiful in the world.

The glittering towers of San Francisco's second world's fair attracted thousands of visitors to the Golden Gate International Exposition in 1939.

Fun of the fair was followed by wartime gloom as World War II began. Because the United States was at war with Japan, the Japanese people of California were taken from their homes and property and sent to camps. Japanese submarines were seen on the coast; one of them shelled Goleta, destroying oil tanks. There were rumors of a Japanese invasion of the Pacific Coast.

40

As the war drew to a close, San Francisco was host to a gathering of representatives of most of the nations of the world. Out of that meeting in 1945 came the United Nations, and so California can rightly claim to be the birthplace of that organization.

In 1948 the world's greatest telescope came to California. The 200-inch (about 508 centimeters) Hale telescope perches on Mt. Palomar, permitting man to peer farther into the mysteries of space than ever before.

Once again a group of travelers became stalled in Donner Pass, where the Donner party was overcome. This time it was the deluxe train, City of San Francisco, that was overwhelmed by heavy snows in the pass in 1952 with 256 passengers and crew. Fortunately, the passengers were rescued with none of the tragedy of that early disaster.

In 1955 the very first national political convention met in California. In 1957 came an even more welcome group, in the opinion of many sport fans. The famed Dodger baseball team left its home in Brooklyn to take up residence in Los Angeles. California now has five major league baseball teams.

As early as 1963, California claimed to have outgrown New York in population; this was confirmed by the 1970 census. More recent events in this busy state have included the general acceptance in 1970 of Cesar Chavez's union, now called the United Farm Workers of America; the Los Angeles earthquake of 1971; and former Governor Ronald Reagan's contest with President Ford for the Republican Presidential nomination in 1976.

Perhaps the most interesting single aspect of California today is the number of racial and ethnic groups, which make California one of the most cosmopolitan of states. The large populations of blacks, Mexican-Americans, and Chinese are well known, but the numbers of other groups are surprising. In Los Angeles County alone live more than 500,000 Canadians and 100,000 Koreans. The many others are illustrated by flourishing newspapers printed in Arabic, Armenian, Danish, Filipino, French, German, Hungarian, Italian, Lithuanian, Swedish, and Spanish.

California can truly claim to be everyone's state.

Natural Treasures

Various areas of the world support different kinds of animals and plants because of their climate and other conditions. These are called "life zones." California has every life zone found on the North American continent except the tropical. There are six different life zones in California. This means that there is a most unusual variety of plants and animals to be found in the state.

Among the many treasures in California, the plant life is probably the most spectacular. Here in one state are the oldest, the biggest, the tallest, and in some cases the smallest!

The oldest living things on earth grow in the Inyo National Forest in the White Mountains. Some of these weird, bent, distorted twists of wood called bristlecone pines are estimated to be four thousand six hundred years old. They grow only about an inch (about 25.4 millimeters) each century. Sometimes when the rainfall has been slight they hardly seem to grow at all, yet they keep on living.

Sometimes all but one small part of the bark of a bristlecone pine will be dead, but that small part continues to nourish the portion of the tree remaining alive.

The largest living things are the giant sequoias of California. These natural wonders can live on almost indefinitely. No one has ever found a giant sequoia dying of old age. Chemicals within them help them resist forest fires and decay. Even trees that have fallen to the ground and died have lain where they fell, for centuries, without decaying. Heavy winds, earthquakes, or something else that causes the tree to tilt or fall are about the only things that kill a sequoia.

The California redwoods are relatives of the sequoia. John Muir, the great naturalist, said, "The redwood is the glory of the Coast Range." Muir did more than anyone else to save these great trees, and today one of the finest groups of redwoods is called Muir Woods National Monument. More than half a million people a year enter this virgin redwood forest.

General Sherman tree in Sequoia National Park.

Carmel on the Pacific Coast.

Sequoias used to grow in many other parts of the world, but they have been unknown elsewhere since the ice age until a few were discovered in China. Other unique trees of California are the famed Monterey pine and Monterey cypress.

Another of the unusual trees is the madrona, made famous in a poem by the well-known writer Bret Harte. One of the most curious of all the trees, the Joshua tree, is really not a tree at all but a kind of yucca plant.

Altogether, there are four thousand kinds of plants native to California. It is noted for its rare lilies and annual flowers.

In just the small area of Point Lobos Reserve State Park, where the Monterey pine and cypress grow, are to be found three hundred species of plants.

The early Spaniards saw a beautiful yellow flower growing everywhere, and they called it the cup of gold. Today their cup of gold is the state flower, the California poppy, only one of the many wildflowers that cover the slopes in spring and attract visitors from all over the world.

Another great floral attraction is the Kruse Rhododendron Reserve where the plants grow 20 or 30 feet (about 6 to 9 meters) high and blossom in late May or early June. Visitors have to go to the

44

channel islands to see still another of the state's famous flowers. This is the giant coreopsis, a treelike kind of sunflower, found only on the islands.

In addition to the native plants, many useful plants have been brought in from other countries, including eucalyptus, pepper trees, and several important kinds of palm trees.

Although there are 178 species of vertebrate animals in California, many of them, such as the California grizzly, have died out or are in danger of become extinct.

Of all the "wild" animals of the state, probably the most appealing and the one most sought by the tourists is the sea lion.

The sea otter, the animal which brought more early visitors to California than any one prize, was so brutally hunted for its fur that it was thought to be extinct. To the delight of nature lovers, several of them were seen a few years ago, and with careful protection their number seems to be increasing.

Another very rare animal, once thought extinct, is the Guadalupe fur seal. A few are now found on Anacapa Island.

Because the Santa Barbara Islands were cut off from the mainland, they have a number of animals that are different from those found anywhere else. Most famous of these is the island fox. Early settlers to the islands brought over sheep and hogs. Now the herds of wild sheep and wild hogs have to be killed as nuisances.

Among the birds of California, the California condor is now one of the most rare, and it is feared that this great bird is becoming extinct.

The Sierra rosy finch, the "silky flycatcher" of the desert, the pygmy owl, and the water ouzel are other birds of interest.

However, the most famous birds of California are the renowned swallows of Capistrano, with their well-timed migrations.

Another famous California migrating creature is not a bird but an insect. Almost every year, visitors can see the beautiful California "butterfly" trees. Thousands of monarch butterflies come to Pacific Grove on the Monterey Peninsula. In their annual migration they swarm across the bay to light on the pines. The trees are so covered that they appear to be in blossom with butterflies.

Both sport and commercial fish are important in California. One of the state's most popular fish is the steelhead, a big seagoing rainbow trout. Each year the steelhead comes in to spawn, but it does not die after spawning as salmon do.

Fisherman may take as many as 25 pounds (about 11.3 kilograms) of surf smelts during the season of April to October. These fish come in to spawn in the sand.

Possibly the most noted of California's sea creatures is the abalone. Sliced into steaks and pounded tender, the meat of the abalone is thought delicious. The beautiful shells were once used by the Indians as money. At one time, the shell was sent to China, where it was made into jewelry and other souvenirs and shipped back to this country for sale.

Fishermen are happy to know that the rare Eagle Lake trout, once near extinction, is making a comeback. Eagle Lake has been called "The Lake That Time Forgot," because the mineralized waters of this support many types of creatures that are only found there.

Among the important commercial fish catches of California waters are sole, turbot, crabs, abalone, shrimp, lobster, clam, squid, oysters, octopus, and salmon.

Gold is still among the minerals to be found in California. The value of the gold, even in the gold rush, was small compared to other more modern minerals, such as petroleum. Natural gas, stone, soda, cement, quicksilver, copper, silver, lead, zinc, platinum, magnesite, chromite, tungsten, silica, pyrites, and many others are found and used commercially.

The state produces most of the world's borax, made famous by the twenty-mule teams, which are no longer used. Borax was formed in California when red hot lava from volcanos flowed into salt lakes.

In many areas, such as Nevada City, quartz mining has gained the greatest importance.

For the nation's most prosperous agricultural state, of course, soil and moisture are particularly important. About one-third of the 100,000,000 acres (about 40,470,000 hectares) in California is suitable for farming. It has been said that almost anything will grow in California if it can be given the water it needs.

A number of plants and animals found in La Brea tar pits are on display at Exposition Park in Los Angeles.

Water is tremendously important, both to crops and to the human and animal populations. Early settlers fought battles, with guns and in the courts, over the rights to water. California and her neighbor states have quarreled about dividing water rights which they share, and these matters often end in the courts.

Each winter a careful check is made of the amount of snow that falls in the mountains. These checks determine how much snow will melt and eventually reach the farms and population centers.

Even the fog is important. In the northern coastal areas—especially around San Francisco—enough moisture is carried by the fogs to supply the needs of truck gardens and to keep the undergrowth flourishing in the forests.

The natural resources of California today are far different from what they were millions of years ago. Remains of life in those far-off days have been preserved in many ways.

Much knowledge of what the prehistoric animals of California must have been like comes from the wonderful La Brea Tar Pits. Over the years, almost every kind of animal and bird has been caught in this sticky tar and preserved by the chemicals for men to see many years later. The La Brea Tar Pits have been called a prehistoric menagerie. Here, among many others, were found the bones of the imperial elephant, the largest of all land mammals; the great ground sloths; and the saber-toothed tigers.

The complete skeleton of an ice-age elephant was found in 1938 near Saltdale. In 1936 a high school student discovered near Patterson the first bones of a dinosaur ever unearthed on the West Coast.

47

People Use Their Treasures

Someone has said that California is not normal if it is not going through some kind of a boom. There have been the booms of fur trading, hides, gold, wheat, railroads, citrus fruit, oil, two world wars, and finally the sonic boom which ushered in the spage-age boom.

LAND OF PLENTY

Agriculture was the first of California's booming businesses, and today it is still going strong. California is the nation's leading agricultural state in dollar value of crops each year, although not in basic agricultural commodities. Annually more than an eight billion-dollar income is received from the state's agricultural products.

California produces 40 percent of all the nation's commercial fruits and nuts, and 25 percent of all the vegetables sold in the United States.

This is far different from the slow and peaceful farming of the Spanish and Mexican rancheros. Yet even in that long-ago day the herds of cattle kept by the ranchers and supported by the grazing lands of California were almost numberless. When the hides of the cattle and the tallow they produced became important, great fortunes were made in that business, and tremendous supplies of these materials poured out even in the early days.

Livestock is important still in California. Cattle and calves, milk and dairy products, poultry and eggs, and sheep and wool all help to feed the growing population.

However, the most valuable single agricultural product is grapes, followed by cotton, hay, and tomatoes. More than two hundred commercial crops are grown in California. Some of these are as little known as cherimoya or as popular as California oranges.

The port of San Francisco is still one of the world's greatest.

California produces enormous quantities of peaches, pears, apricots, olives, figs, lemons, avocados, walnuts, almonds, barley, dried lima beans, plums, sweet cherries, dates, and nectarines, usually leading the nation in these. Other important crops are lettuce, potatoes, peas, sugar beets, and cantaloupe.

As early as 1873, Isabella Bird wrote, "We drove to the ferry through the streets of San Francisco, with sidewalks heaped with thousands of cantaloupe and watermelon, tomatoes, cucumbers, squashes, pears, grapes, peaches, apricots—all of startling size as compared with any I ever saw before."

The Coachella Valley produces 90 percent of all American dates. Here are found the thickest groves of fruit-bearing palm trees in the hemisphere. Date palms are among the oldest trees cultivated by man, yet they were not introduced into this country until 1900, under the leadership of James "Tama Jim" Wilson, the United States Secretary of Agriculture.

One unusual type of farming is the growing of brussels sprouts, centered at Santa Cruz.

Watsonville is called the strawberry capital of the world. Another "world center" is Castroville, which holds the claim as artichoke center of the world. The only large-scale cultivation of artichokes in the United States is found in this region.

California citrus orchards owe their beginning to the first orange grove, which was set out at San Gabriel mission near Los Angeles in 1804. Then in 1873, Eliza C. Tibbetts of Riverside managed to get cuttings of a new type of orange tree from Brazil. This was the beginning of the navel orange industry in the United States. The "Parent Navel Orange," one of the original trees, can still be seen at Riverside. The world's first citrus fair was held at Riverside in 1879.

Another interesting and unusual agricultural business is based on the growing of flowers for their seed. The Lompoc Valley is the world's biggest center of commercial flower-seed production.

Capitola is labeled the begonia capital of the United States. There begonias 10 inches (250 millimeters) across are common. An ounce (about 28 grams) of their seed can be worth as much as several thousand dollars.

The state's great business in grapes, wines, and raisins sprang from the first vineyard planted by the Franciscans at the Mission San Diego de Alcalá in 1770.

Fresno County, California, claims to have the greatest agricultural output of any single county in the United States.

Another agricultural claim of California is that it has the country's highest rate of horsepower per farm, coming from the millions of tractors and other agricultural engines and implements which lighten the farmers' burdens throughout the state.

Apparently about the only agricultural venture that ever failed in California was the plan of Martin Seely to use monkeys as fruit pickers at Santa Clara.

The greatest single problem for agriculture in California is water for the crops. Many dry or desert areas of the state only need irrigation to become gardens.

Even the early Spanish missions brought in water from long distances by aqueduct for irrigation. The mission at San Diego created California's first aqueduct.

An Englishman, Thomas Blythe, had a plan for turning the valley of the Colorado River into another Nile, but nothing much was done along these lines until modern times. Congressman Phil Swing sponsored a bill to place a dam across the mighty Colorado River, and in 1936 the Hoover Dam was completed. By 1938 the "All American Canal" was bringing water made available from the dam reservoir from the eastern border clear across the state.

Today, vast projects are completed or under way to wring out and conserve for human needs every drop of water possible. The Oroville Dam, world's largest and highest earth-fill dam, is designed to carry water as far as San Diego.

Because more water falls in the north, great efforts will be made to bring other northern water to the parched south. Shasta Dam makes it possible for water falling on remote Mount Shasta to travel as much as 500 miles (about 804 kilometers) to Bakersfield.

Shasta Dam is the world's second largest concrete structure, and its tremendous lake can store as much as 9,000 gallons (about 34,000 liters) of water for every person in the United States.

THE BETTER TO MAKE THINGS WITH

California manufactures thirty billion dollars worth of new products every year. This includes transportation equipment (aircraft, automobiles, ships), food products, electrical and electronic machinery, fabricated metal products, non-electrical machinery, chemicals, printing and publishing, primary metals, stone, clay and glass, lumber and wood products, petroleum products, rubber products, apparel, and furniture.

This great outpouring of products is a far cry from the quiet early days when each mission had a weaving room, a blacksmith shop, a tannery, wine press, warehouses, brick making, pottery making, soap making, candlemaking, and some method of grinding corn.

Just before the American conquest of California, the area was shipping out a large quantity of lumber, soap, and brandy.

Stephen Smith set up the first steam grist and sawmill at Bodega in 1843. Sutter's mill, where gold was later found, was one of the earliest manufacturing "complexes." In addition to grinding grain and cutting timber, Sutter's establishment manufactured coarse woven blankets and operated a distillery.

By 1860, there were one hundred grist mills and three hundred sawmills operating in California. San Francisco was the center for refining sugar from the raw sugar shipped from Hawaii.

A machine used for harvesting lettuce.

California's wine industry dates back to 1839-40, when the state's first winery was established by Tiburcia Tapia at Cucamonga. This was the second oldest winery in the United States. Today, California leads the states in production of wine.

Another grape-based industry was founded by the noted Hungarian authority on grapes, A. Haraszthy. He started the raisin industry in California by bringing in the muscat-alexandria grapes in 1851. Today California leads in the production of all kinds of dried fruits, with the industry centered at San Jose.

California is also the national leader in frozen fruits and vegetables.

The state has been foremost in the organization of fruit and vegetable growers into cooperatives for the processing and marketing of their products, and now many important and well-known fruit and vegetable cooperatives have their headquarters in California.

Hydroelectric power was first generated in California at Etiwanda in 1882. By the year 1899, California industries included meat packing, sugar and molasses refineries, lumber mills, brickyards, flour and grist mills, fruit and vegetable canneries, foundries, and machine shops.

One of California's early industrialists became internationally famous, and has given his name to the language in a word which is used all around the world. In 1850 Levi Strauss sailed "around the Horn" on the long, hard voyage to California.

Mr. Strauss' baggage included a bundle of very heavy fabrics which he intended to use for making tents. These he had planned to sell for a grubstake to the mines.

Instead, a miner persuaded Strauss to make him a pair of pants from the material. The story is told that because Strauss did not have the right thread for the pockets and other points of strain, he used rivets. Soon more and more miners were calling for those riveted work trousers of Levi's, and Mr. Strauss never reached the gold fields. He began to manufacture his Levi's, and today the name is a trade-marked household word. Levi Strauss and Company still operates out of San Francisco, making Levi's and many other kinds of garments.

California prepared for the missile age by its pioneering in the field of aviation. The plane used by Charles Lindbergh in his famous solo Atlantic hop in 1927 was made by Ryan Aeronautical at San Diego. This and many other famous made-in-California aircraft forecast the state's supremacy in aviation manufacture. The process was speeded by such moves as that made by Consolidated Aircraft Corporation from Buffalo, New York, to San Diego, California, in 1935.

San Diego pioneered in aviation at a much earlier date. As far back as 1883 John J. Montgomery made his first controlled wing glider flight, and Glen Curtiss took off from the waters near San Diego in 1911 in the world's first successful seaplane test flight.

These small beginnings have grown until California now has the country's largest concentration of the aerospace industry. The people who had built the most airplanes were able to adapt themselves most easily to making missiles. Missile and space activities bring more than a billion dollars to California each year.

California is also one of the leaders in the field of electronics, with a large part of the industry centered in the San Francisco Bay area.

SHADOWS THAT MADE HISTORY

Large and important as are the great industries of California, the business that has made it most famous has a product little more substantial to show for its efforts than a shadow on a screen.

Hollywood was a quiet residential suburb, until in 1911 a motion picture company came there for the first time. This was the David H. Nestor Film Company, which produced Hollywood's first motion picture in a studio at Sunset Boulevard and Gower Street.

From then on, it must have seemed to the residents of Hollywood that movie people were dropping out of the sky, they came so fast.

In fact, one movie figure did drop out of the sky on Hollywood. Pearl White, a heroine in many movie thrillers, was doing some scenes in a prop balloon when it suddenly broke away and soared up into the air. Miss White quickly drifted out toward the sea but pulled the cord to deflate the balloon just in time to keep herself from floating away over the ocean. This was one of the first times that a Holly-wood celebrity had made headlines, but not the last.

Hollywood was not, however, the first California town to produce a motion picture. In 1908, the Count of Monte Cristo was made in Los Angeles. This was the first commercial motion picture made in California.

It was not long before Hollywood became the center of the motion picture industry and by 1930 motion pictures had grown to be one of the ten largest industries in the United States.

All over the world, the name Hollywood meant movies.

Because of the many stars and personalities available there, Holly-wood also became a center for the radio and television industry. The first regular radio broadcasts of speech and music in California began at San Jose over station KQW. In 1915 the station broadcast the ukulele tunes of Al and Clarence Pearce. Al Pearce remained a popular performer for many years.

The coming of radio added to the movies' success, but when television brought a motion picture into almost every American home, the movie industry began to suffer, and it has been forced to make many changes. Hollywood has lost much of its glamor as foreign film makers have grown more important and as American stars and producers have moved abroad.

TREASURES POUR FROM THE EARTH

Each year the mineral wealth of California adds more than two bil-lion dollars to the income of her people. Petroleum, natural gas, building stone, sand and gravel, cement, gold, borates, zinc, lead, mercury, and iron ore all are important minerals.

Gold, of course, was the mineral that put California on the map of the world. The lure of gold brought far more wealth to the state than the actual worth of the gold itself. In all the years gold has been worked in California it has produced only two and a half billion dol-lars of income. But the gold rush brought an almost instant popula-tion and created a demand for goods and services.

Walt Disney's creations added to Hollywood's international reputation.

The first gold seekers tried only the crudest methods, but by 1851 a mill for crushing gold quartz was in operation. The year 1852 was the largest single gold year in California history, with eighty-one million dollars of gold produced.

Hydraulic mining, where the soil was washed away by powerful streams of water, had been introduced in 1852. Hydraulic mining damaged the land and the rivers; it ruined farms and filled up rivers and harbors with sludge. In 1880 hydraulic mining was banned.

The most valuable gold in California was found in what is called the Mother Lode. This is quartz rock in which the gold is mixed. Colonel John C. Frémont was one of the first to see the immense possibilities of extracting gold from the quartz rock. He built quartz-crushing mills and operated them day and night.

The famous Mother Lode of California runs down through the foothill counties of California from north of the American River and dies out not far south of Mariposa.

The gold of the Golden State is still adding to California's wealth, but only a small amount is taken out each year. Today the real gold of California is "black gold." California usually ranks among the top three producing states in petroleum. Natural gas also brings in a large income supplying energy needs.

The friars at the missions used California's oil and tar in a few simple ways. Even before that, the Indians found some uses for the surface oils. The state's first successful drilling for oil took place in 1859. By the year 1866, 40,000 to 50,000 gallons (about 150,000 to 190,000 liters) of oil were produced, and then the backers gave the matter up as impractical.

In 1874 California Star Oil Company built the first refinery in the state, near Newhall. By 1888 annual oil production in California had risen to 690,000 barrels (about 110 million liters). In 1919 oil was the most important industry of the state.

In 1880, San Bernardino County was the only place in the United States where tin was being mined in commercial quantities.

GETTING AROUND

Transportation and communication have always been important to Californians. Over the King's Highway (El Camino Real), the first road between the missions, soldier couriers carried the mail; squeaking carts with solid oak wheels groaned and lumbered over the ruts and boulders. Trains of pack mules made their leisurely way. Over the years this became one of the most fabled trails in history—the Golden Road.

In 1829 a new route was opened to overland travel when Antonia Armijo opened the Old Spanish Trail stretching from Santa Fe to Los Angeles.

During the gold rush, desperate travelers took almost any chance on whatever transportation might be offered. In addition to the overland route, many easteners took a boat to Panama, went across the Isthmus of Panama by railroad, then took another ship to California. Twenty-nine steamships of the Pacific Mail Steamship Company stopped at the terminal of the Panama Railroad. In only ten years those ships carried the unbelievable total of 175,000 passengers and 200 million dollars in gold.

The famous Clipper ships, made especially for their speed, sailed clear around the Horn to bring the gold seekers to San Francisco.

The Golden Gate Bridge, an architectural wonder, was completed in 1937.

In San Francisco Bay, ferryboating began as early as 1851 in a converted whaleboat. Before the Bay Bridge opened, the ferryboats had become what were often referred to as "Floating Palaces."

Inland steamers carried prospectors and traders up the Sacramento and San Joaquin rivers, and even a few sailing vessels tried the hazardous voyage upriver.

The names of the Adams Express Company and Wells Fargo became well known in the shipment of goods and valuables.

Then came the railroads. The first railroad was the Sacramento Valley Line, from the capital to Folsom.

When Theodore Judah found a route suitable for a railroad across the Sierra Nevadas, California at last became linked with quick and efficient transportation directly to the east.

Because many parts of the state were not reached by rail, California became one of the pioneers in the development of truck transportation, and buses became as popular on the highways as the rumbling stagecoaches had been a century before.

San Francisco pioneered in transportation of another kind. In order to solve the problem of carrying people over the steep hills, the city created the first cable-car street railway system in the world in 1873, and the cable cars are still one of the greatest attractions of the Bay City.

Some of the world's finest airports are found in California, which is not surprising in light of the state's early leadership in the air.

As early as 1883 John J. Montgomery, Professor of Physics at the University of Santa Clara, soared to the remarkable height of 600 feet (about 182 meters) in the first controlled wing flight ever made. Silas Christofferson made the first non-stop flight from San Francisco to Los Angeles in 1914.

The vast world of the Pacific opened up in a new way when the first China Clipper flight was made on a round trip from San Francisco to Manila.

Today, California is America's gateway to Hawaii and the regions of the Pacific, both by sea and by air. In order to open up the Los Angeles area to the great ocean-going vessels of the world, the Port of Los Angeles has spent 155 million dollars in the improvement of the harbor at San Pedro. The 11,000 foot (about 3,350 meters) breakwater was constructed and the inner harbor excavated in 1910.

Still another great development in water transportation was the opening in 1963 of the deep-water channel for 43 miles (about 69 kilometers) to bring ocean ships to Sacramento by way of Suisun Bay. This was designed to make Sacramento once more a major port and provide for expansion of the city as a port over a period of many years.

SO MUCH TO DO

Lumbering, banking, fishing, publishing, and many other activities occupy the people of California.

California is the home of the largest commercial bank in the world, the Bank of America, with headquarters at San Francisco. And San Francisco is generally considered the nation's second-greatest banking center.

Throughout its history, the lumber of the state has been important. Early Californians were careless with their precious trees. The Indians set fires annually to clear out the underbrush, and only the almost-fireproof redwood trees survived. Gold miners destroyed the forests, and cattlemen set forest fires to clear the land for grazing. But today the forest lands are protected, and scientific lumbering permits the forests to renew themselves. The great redwood trees are still giving their wonderful wood for the uses of man, but only mature or felled trees are being used, so that the future yield is protected, and of course the state and national groves are entirely protected.

Dr. Robert Semple published the first newspaper in California, in 1846. The newspaper was only a single sheet. The publishers could not obtain any paper, so they finally printed their newspaper on the wrapping paper that had been used to ship packages of cigarettes. A large crowd was waiting to get the first issue of this first newspaper. Half the paper was printed in English, the other half in Spanish.

When he was a young man, one of the state's most famous newspapermen took over his father's *San Francisco Examiner* in 1887. This was the famous William Randolph Hearst, who built a publishing empire.

Los Angeles harbor at San Pedro is headquarters for one of the largest commercial fishing fleets in the world. A large part of California's fishing industry was disrupted when the sardines disappeared. Sardine fishing reached its peak in 1936 when 1.5 billion pounds (about 680 million kilograms) of sardines were caught and packed. Monterey's fisheries were credited with the largest commercial catch in the western hemisphere.

No one knows for sure why the sardines disappeared, but possibly changes in currents or water temperature were responsible. Cannery Row, made famous by writer John Steinbeck, now is a tourist attraction.

Whaling is no longer important as it once was, either, but visitors may still see large whales coming through the Golden Gate, nestled under the whale boats that have captured and killed them.

Retail sales in California now total the enormous sum of more than fifty billion dollars per year.

No account of California's commercial activities could fail to mention tourists. Ever since the early rail excursions, tourists have been adding significantly to the state's business wealth. From the very beginning, many tourists have been so pleased with the state that they have made California their permanent home. Today the billions of dollars of tourist income are among the state's most important revenue sources.

60

Human Treasures

THE "FATHER" OF CALIFORNIA

In 1931, California was asked to name the two most prominent people in its history so that their statues could be placed in the Hall of Fame in the Capitol at Washington. One of those chosen was Miguel José Serra, better known as Father Junipero Serra, who is usually considered the founder of California.

Father Serra found only wilderness in California. He was far away from all civilization. But with scarcely more than determination he founded the San Diego Mission on the shores of San Diego Bay. Less than a year later he founded San Carlos Mission in Monterey. A year later he established San Antonio de Padua.

After only another two months, San Gabriel Arcángel Mission came into being under his guidance, followed a year later by Mission San Luis Obispo.

Within three years, Father Serra had placed five flourishing centers of civilization where only wilderness had stood before. Buildings had been built; natives had been converted and brought in to help with the work. Agriculture, grazing, and other necessary activities had begun. This must be considered a great accomplishment.

Altogether, Father Serra founded nine of the twenty-one missions in California. He remained father-president of the California missions for fifteen years.

Santa Ines Mission,
founded September, 1804.

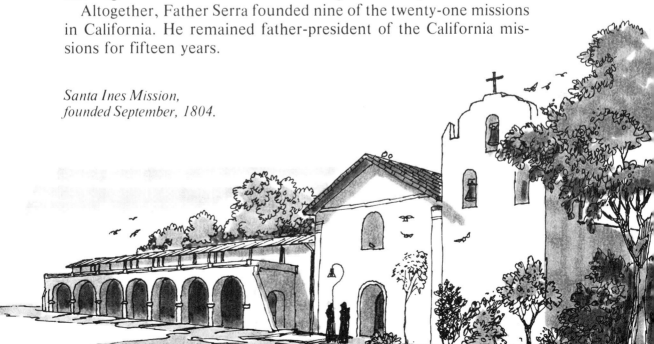

He did his work in spite of poor health that might have confined many people to their beds. He had a severe ulcer on his leg, which never healed; he suffered from asthma, and had a cancer of the skin. But the "Long Gown" continued to be active until his death in 1784. When he died, he was regarded so highly that the people tried to obtain pieces of his robe as holy relics.

Those who come to Mission San Carlos Borromeo de Carmelo, where Father Serra had his headquarters, may see the grave where the founder of California rests today.

TWO EARLY CALIFORNIANS

John Sutter had failed at everything he had tried before he came to California. He was a native of Switzerland, and became the first white man to settle in the interior of the state. We have seen how in 1839 he founded the Swiss colony that he called New Helvetia, the beginning of modern Sacramento.

He made great claims about his ability and experiences as a soldier, and about his wealth and authority, but many people considered him to be something of a fraud.

He claimed 97,000 acres (about 39,000 hectares) in California's great central valley and lived in truly grand style. He even set up private fortifications with twenty-four cannon for protection.

It was on his property that the gold of California was first found. However, Sutter and his associates were not able to protect their interests in the wild rush for gold that followed. Instead of making them rich, the gold strike made it impossible for them to carry out the many enterprises. Sutter is supposed to have said that he was ruined by the gold rush that made so many others wealthy.

There was also tragedy in the life of John C. Frémont. When Frémont came to California, he was a United States army captain, but the United States would not admit that Captain Frémont and his party had been sent for any other purpose than exploring. The United States Government was embarrassed when Fremont fortified a little hill in California and raised the American flag.

Later, after the war with Mexico, Frémont was court-martialed for insubordination because of his actions during the war. He was found guilty, but most Californians did not think he was guilty. They showed their confidence by choosing him as one of the first two United States senators from California. He was the son-in-law of Senator Thomas Hart Benton, who was one of the strongest friends of western expansion.

By 1856, Colonel Frémont's fame had grown so that he was the first candidate for the Presidency ever nominated by the Republican Party. Because Frémont lost the election, many experts feel that the coming of the Civil War was delayed. If Frémont had won, it is thought that the South would have broken away at that time rather than later.

John C. Frémont purchased 44,000 acres (about 17,800 hectares) of a Spanish grant in Mariposa County. This is often considered the most valuable single piece of real estate ever owned by one individual. However, Frémont could not gain clear title to the property and the Spanish right to sell the land was contested in the courts.

The matter went through the California courts, the United States Land Commissioners, and finally after ten years, to the United States Supreme Court. The costs were tremendous. Colonel Fremont was in debt because of his expenses in running for the Presidency and losses incurred by a bad business manager. By the time the Supreme Court decided in his favor, he owed more than a half-million dollars.

The story of his property does have a happy ending, however. When his title was secure, he sold the property to a New York banker, receiving, it is said, a million and a half in cash and a portion of stock in the new company.

Frémont was the discoverer or explorer of a great part of California, under the guidance of his scout, the noted Kit Carson.

As Frémont looked out across San Francisco Bay to the harbor entrance one day, the sun was just setting in the west, and it shed a golden glow. "This is the 'Golden Gate,'" Frémont exclaimed, and it has been the Golden Gate ever since.

A CREATIVE CLIMATE

The climate, scenery, and people of California have always seemed to appeal to writers and to inspire them.

Mark Twain went to California as a young man and picked up the characters and backgrounds for many of his most successful works. *The Celebrated Jumping Frog of Calaveras County and Other Sketches* appeared in 1867 and was his first great success. Some have called this work the beginning of the "California school" of writing.

Another famous writer, Bret Harte, worked as a California newspaperman. In 1868 *The Luck of Roaring Camp* brought him fame.

Helen Hunt Jackson's famous book *Ramona* appeared in 1884. It dealt with the terrible treatment of the Indians by the white man. *Ramona* has been called a second *Uncle Tom's Cabin* because of the effect it had on the general relations between Indian and the white man.

Jack London has been labeled California's most spectacular and widely read author. His grave near Santa Rosa is now the site of Jack London Historical State Park.

When Edwin Markham's *The Man With the Hoe* was published, it is said to have made him famous in a day.

C. H. Miller, who was generally known as Joaquin Miller, was one of the best-known early California poets. He died in Oakland in 1913.

The *History of the Pacific States of North America*, by Hubert Howe Bancroft, in twenty-eight volumes, is considered by some experts to be the greatest feat of history in modern times.

Upton Sinclair, Ambrose Bierce—who disappeared in Mexico just before World War I—and Robinson Jeffers were other noted California men of letters.

Famous modern writers of California include John Steinbeck, native of Pacific Grove; William Saroyan, born in San Joaquin Valley; and Robert Frost, who is not usually associated with California but was a Californian by birth. Gertrude Stein spent her girlhood in the San Francisco Bay region.

Noted authors of other countries have visited California. Robert Louis Stevenson lived in California in 1879 and was married there. He is supposed to have used Point Lobos as the model for Spyglass Hill in *Treasure Island.* Another English writer, Rudyard Kipling, came to California in 1889.

Among California's noted composers are Charles Wakefield Cadman, William Grant Still, and Ernst Bacon, who won the Pulitzer Prize in 1932 for his *Symphony in D Minor.*

THE BIG FOUR

In the early 1860s, four wealthy Sacramento merchants, Leland Stanford, Collis P. Huntington, Charles Crocker, and Mark Hopkins, became interested in building a railroad across the continent. Stanford, who was then governor of California, broke ground for the western end of the transcontinental railroad in 1862. In 1869 he drove the golden spike that celebrated the completion of the route.

James Marshall was building this mill for Captain Sutter when he found gold in the tailrace on January 24, 1848.

As the wealth and power of the western portion of the transcontinental railroad grew, the authority of the four owners was also growing. They came to be known as the Big Four. Their railroad, since known as the Southern Pacific, was often called the "Octopus."

Some of the Big Four were also known for their philanthropy. This was particularly true of Leland Stanford, whose contributions to Stanford University and the arts are perhaps better known than the stories of greed and suppression often charged to the Big Four.

PEOPLE TO MATCH A GREAT LAND

An almost endless list of native-born Californians, or people who have been closely associated with the state, have gained wide reputation. Only a few of these can be mentioned.

California fame was gained by the Indian Chief Sequoya. Chief Sequoya gave his name to the giant sequoia trees; in 1821 the chief was responsible for one of the unique feats of scholarship of its kind. He completed the first alphabet of an Indian language.

The first native-born Californian to become governor of the state under the United States Government was Romualdo Pacheco, who took office in 1875. It was not until 1893 that a native-born Californian was chosen to serve his state in the United States Senate. This was Stephen M. White. He has been called the Father of the Los Angeles harbor.

William C. Ralston and the Gianini family gained fame as bankers. Lillian Gilbreth, a native of Oakland, became world renowned as the mother in the book, play, and motion picture *Cheaper by the Dozen.* However, Mrs. Gilbreth already had an international reputation as an efficiency engineer.

The only California-born President of the United States was Richard M. Nixon, born in Yorba Linda in 1913. Though not a native of California, President Herbert Hoover kept many associations with the state, especially in connection with Stanford University. Earl Warren was a long-time governor of California and Chief Justice of the United States.

Luther Burbank, the famous plant wizard, carried out his experiments at his headquarters in Santa Rosa, and he is buried under a cedar of Lebanon tree in his garden.

Three California electronic pioneers were Dr. Lee de Forest, inventor of the audion tube, Herbert Van Etten, and Charles V. Longwood. These three teamed together at Palo Alto to make important discoveries in electronics.

In nearby Oakland, Henry J. Kaiser built the headquarters of his industrial empire. Another prominent California industrialist was the sugar-refining millionaire, John D. Spreckels. He was greatly responsible for the development of San Diego and was personally credited with the creation of a railroad that was said to be impossible to build, over the mountains eastward from San Diego.

UNUSUAL PERSONALITIES

In 1905 Walter E. Scott began to spend great sums of money on elaborate projects. He built a $2,000,000 castle in Death Valley and lived in great luxury there. He once chartered a train to try to beat the transcontinental train crossing record and became one of the most popular mystery figures of his day. The mystery lay in the fact that the real source of his wealth was not known, although he hinted that it came from a hidden mine. Finally, a Chicago millionaire became known as the real source of his hidden wealth. He had carried on this expensive and apparently pointless support of Scotty for many years, for some never fully explained reason.

Another personality of California whose name was world-renowned was the evangelist Aimee Semple McPherson.

No account of the personalities of California would be complete without mention of those whose acting, directing, and producing made Hollywood known throughout the world—such names as D. W. Griffith, Cecil B. de Mille, Louis B. Mayer, Rudolph Valentino, Gloria Swanson, Charlie Chaplin, Mary Pickford, Douglas Fairbanks, Sr., Will Rogers, Clark Gable, Marilyn Monroe, and others.

Left: The library tower at San Diego State College. Above: The rose garden in Exposition Park at the University of Southern California, Los Angeles. Below: The Palomar Observatory, built by the California Institute of Technology.

Teaching and Learning

Many authorities have said that California has the finest educational system in the world, when considered as a whole, from kindergarten to graduate study. Possibly this is so because California always spends a large percentage of its state taxes on education.

The university of the Pacific at Stockton was founded in 1851 by the Reverend Isaac Owen, as California Wesleyan College, a Methodist school.

Another college founded in 1851 was Santa Clara College, now the University of Santa Clara. It was organized by the Jesuit Fathers.

The ten campuses of the University of California combine to form the largest university complex in the United States. This present stature sprang from a humble beginning in 1868 on the campus of the College of California. The first twelve graduates of the University of California finished their studies in 1873, and the university moved to its present campus at Berkeley.

This is still the principal campus. In 1923 it was almost completely destroyed by fire but was quickly rebuilt. It expanded to other sites and now is considered one of the great universities of the world.

Leland Stanford, Junior, University, founded at Palo Alto in 1891, is one of the country's outstanding privately supported universities. Its branches in Germany, Italy, France, Taiwan, and Japan make it a truly international institution.

Stanford came into being when the Leland Stanfords set aside a part of their great estate to become a university in memory of their son. Later, all of the land in the Palo Alto estate of the Stanfords was granted to the university.

President Herbert Hoover's close association with Stanford is remembered in the Hoover Institute and Library.

The Stanford Research Institute is the largest applied research organization in the country.

In 1880 the University of Southern California was founded under Methodist leadership and has become widely recognized.

Because of its excellence, study at the California Institute of Technology is the goal of young scientists from all over the world.

Yosemite Falls in Yosemite National Park.

Enchantment of California

ONE OF THE MOST FAVORED SPOTS

The visitor who gets his first glimpse of California by sailing into San Diego Bay is doing exactly what the discoverer of California, Cabrillo, did so many years ago. And one of the first things to attract the visitor's attention might be the Cabrillo National Monument at the tip of Point Loma.

Neither Cabrillo nor Father Serra, who founded San Diego in 1769, would recognize much of the area today. But present-day residents would still agree with the great naturalist, Louis Agassiz, who called San Diego one of the most favored spots on earth and spoke of its genial and healthful atmosphere.

San Diego boasts of the "shortness" of its thermometer, which never moves very far toward either extreme heat or extreme cold.

At one time the city was famous for its trade in cattle hides, its fandangos, rodeos, and bull and bear fights. Today its fame rests on its large and growing industry, its zoo, said to be the largest in the world, the great United States Naval Base, and other attractions.

The San Diego Zoo began as a small menagerie left over from the world's fair in 1915. It was built into its present greatness in the world of animals by Dr. Harry Wegeforth. Beautiful Balboa Park where the zoo is located also contains wonderful landscaping, art galleries, museums, and theaters.

Another Balboa Park attraction is the Spreckels Outdoor Organ, also a San Diego claim as world's largest.

At La Jolla, a popular section of San Diego, is one of the leading scientific institutions of its kind, Scripps Institution of Oceanography, with its aquarium and museum.

Another major military establishment in the San Diego vicinity is Camp Pendleton, at Oceanside, the largest of all Marine bases.

In the northern part of San Diego County, peering through the clear air of Mt. Palomar, is the great 200-inch (about 508 centimeters) telescope, second largest in the world. Mt. Wilson is the site of another renowned observatory.

MORE THAN JUST SAND

Across the state from San Diego is the desert land of Imperial County. In the heart of the county lies a valley, now so green and productive that it is hard to imagine it was once the same desert land as the rest. This, of course, is extraordinary Imperial Valley. Irrigation has made it one of the great fruit and vegetable gardens of America. In Imperial Valley, El Centro is the largest town in the United States below sea level.

Not far away is an area that was a dry lake until 1905. In that year the Colorado River flooded the old lake bed, and the Salton Sea has been there ever since. At present, the Salton Sea State Park is being developed as one of the major recreational areas of the state.

West of the Salton Sea is a picturesque land known as Anza-Borrego Desert State Park. Here stretches a half-million acres (about 200,000 hectares) of raw desert wilderness, preserved in its natural state, with few roads. In spring this seemingly foresaken land blossoms with the beauty of 600 species of desert flowers, scattered among the weird elephant trees.

Not far from the elephant trees may be found the camels. These are the camels that race at Indio in the only camel races in the United States. Indio is also the home of the National Date Festival.

Only a few miles from Indio is Palm Springs, often called America's foremost desert resort, founded in 1876.

Before Palm Springs became a valuable property, the government sent the Indians out there to what appeared to be a foresaken country. With the popularity of their land as a resort, the Indians have prospered—fortunately and unexpectedly. Where almost no water was to be found, there are now thousands of swimming pools, and millions of people visit this once desolate land every year.

To the north, still mostly desert country, is the largest county in the United States, San Bernardino County. The city of San Bernardino, shut off from the desert by the San Bernardino Mountains, was the first Anglo-Saxon community in California. It was founded in 1851 by a group of Mormons who bought Rancho San Bernardino and laid out a city similar to Salt Lake City.

One of the world's scenic drives is the Rim-o-the-World Highway between San Bernardino and Big Bear Lake. This is the region of the famed natural "arrowhead." The Arrowhead landmark is formed by a natural growth of vegetation in the shape of an arrowhead, which points in the direction of Hot Springs. Lake Arrowhead is a popular winter resort.

In nearby Joshua Tree National Monument, those ghostly relatives of the yucca plant raise their many arms into the sky. Because of these upraised branches, that reminded them of Joshua praying, the Mormons gave the "trees" their name.

In the Mojave Desert to the north lies Barstow. Nearby is Inscription Canyon, where the Indians carved their sign language in long-ago days. At Barstow may be seen the restored ghost town of Calico near the Calico Mountains. This was recreated by private funds in 1950. From this area silver worth eighty-six million dollars was taken in the short space of fifteen years.

Still farther north is one of California's best-known areas. Here a group of gold hunters of 1849 were hopelessly lost in the searing salt flats, which gave the place its evil name—Death Valley. It is hard to realize that this dry area was an inland sea millions of years ago. Here the famous twenty-mule teams raised choking clouds of chemical dust as they hauled out the borax, which had been mined in the awful heat. This heat once reached 134 degrees Fahrenheit (56.7 degrees Celsius), just under the world's record.

Today Death Valley is a national monument. The valley is 140 miles (about 225 kilometers) long and up to 16 miles (about 25 kilometers) wide. At its lowest point, 280 feet (about 85 meters) below sea level, it is the lowest spot on the North American continent. The Devil's Golf Course, a natural bridge, and Scotty's Castle are all found in Death Valley.

MEN AMONG THE ANGELS

El Pueblo de Nuestra Señora Le Reina de Los Angeles de Porciuncula was founded in California in 1781 by Governor Don Felipe de

Neve, and the world has never been quite the same since. In the time since its founding, the City of Our Lady of the Angels has become one of the most talked about anywhere.

For the visitor interested in early days, the oldest section of Los Angeles, the Olvera Street area, is being preserved and restored. Here is found the oldest house in Los Angeles, Avila Adobe.

Each of the eleven families who first settled Los Angeles was given a lot facing a plaza. The plaza remained the center of the town for almost a century. Throughout the Spanish and Mexican periods, Los Angeles continued to be a sleepy, ugly town. When the Americans and gold came at about the same time, and Los Angeles could make a fortune by selling cattle to supply the needs of the gold hunters, the town came to life and has more than proved its liveliness in the years since.

The city's modern history and its rapid growth began in 1892 with the first oil well strike within the city limits. At the beginning of the century, fewer than 200,000 people lived in the Los Angeles area. Today there are 7,000,000.

Because Los Angeles is so spread out, it has been called the world's most decentralized metropolis. It is scattered over an area of 450 square miles (about 1,165 square kilometers). Millions of tourists visit here yearly and spend many millions of dollars.

Almost every kind of attraction imaginable brings visitors and permanent residents to the Los Angeles area. Important to both visitors and residents is the vast industry of the area, which has been called the "Industrial Center of the West, strong arm in defense of the United States and a center of the space age effort."

One of the greatest tourist attractions in the world was created by a leading Hollywood figure, Walt Disney, who made Disneyland, at Anaheim, a place where "the present does not exist, only the past and the future."

Another prominent amusement area has come a long way from the fruit stand that the Knotts family set up on their berry farm. The family's imagination and their operation grew until Knotts Berry Farm has become one of the best-known establishments in America. Their recreation of a gold rush town is one of the finest.

At San Marino is the Huntington Library, Art Gallery, and gardens. Here visitors may see one of the most popular pictures in the world, "The Blue Boy" by Gainsborough, also the painting "Pinkie" by Thomas Lawrence. Among the rare books are a Gutenberg Bible and a first folio of Shakespeare. Here also is said to be the world's largest cactus garden.

To assure its position in the arts, Los Angeles has constructed a mammoth music center as a rival of New York's Lincoln Center.

California's most famous mission, San Juan Capistrano, is a link with the Spanish missionaries who planted civilization in California even though their backs were constantly to a wilderness. The famous swallows of Capistrano leave it faithfully on St. John's Day, October 23, and return with clockwork precision on St. Joseph's Day, March 19. No one has been able to explain successfully this miraculous timing ability.

Father Serra is honored by a cross on the peak of Mt. Rubidoux at Riverside. The World Peace Tower is on the same mountain.

At Whittier stands a monument to another prominent early Californian, Pio Pico, last Mexican Governor of California. This is his mansion, which has been restored.

Offshore from the Los Angeles area are the Channel Islands, part of which are now included in the Channel Islands National Monument. Most famous of the Channel Islands is Santa Catalina, long owned by the Wrigley family of gum and baseball fame. Santa Catalina was discovered by Cabrillo. In 1834 it experienced a brief gold rush, and now is principally a tourist attraction. The Wrigley family donated their vast holdings on Santa Catalina to Los Angeles County Department of Parks and Recreation, and Santa Catalina is now the county's largest park.

Pacific Palisades is the site of Will Rogers State Park, where the estate of one of America's great humorists has been preserved by the people, in his honor.

At Arcadia, the renowned Los Angeles State and County Arboretum displays rare plants from all parts of the world.

To many millions of Americans, the name Pasadena means the Tournament of Roses and the Rose Bowl game. The first Rose

The Rose Bowl parade in Pasadena.

parade at Pasadena in 1890 was a procession of decorated carriages. Easterners were so pleased with the idea of roses in January that a Tournament of Roses Association was formed in 1898, and the tournament has been one of America's best-known annual attractions ever since. The modern history of the bowl game as we know it today began in 1916, although one game was played in 1902 between Stanford and Michigan. Michigan won 49 to 0. The bowl itself was constructed in 1912.

COASTING ALONG

Between Los Angeles and San Francisco lies one of the most interesting areas of the United States, especially along the coast. Clinging to the coast most of the way is state highway number one, which has been called The Wonderful One. The Pacific Ocean is said to have one of its calmest stretches around Santa Barbara; but the earth there was not so calm in 1925, when an earthquake destroyed most of the city. Santa Barbara took advantage of this disaster to rebuild in a very unique way. Everything was planned to return to the old Spanish style of architecture. Even the railroad roundhouse was patterned after a Spanish bull ring.

Mission Santa Barbara was often given the title Queen of the Missions.

The Moreton Bay fig tree is said to be the largest in the United States. Planted in 1877, its branches spread for 149 feet (about 45 meters). Ten thousand people could stand in its shade at noon.

Most visitors who proceed along the coast sooner or later are struck by the fact that California has been particularly foresighted in saving a large number of the best beaches on the Pacific as state parks, so that these wonderful recreational areas are preserved.

One of the great tourist attractions of the coast is the region of almond orchards around Paso Robles. In the early spring the earth appears to be boiling over with blooming trees.

Also at Paso Robles are the famous hot springs, used from Indian times. Even the grizzly bears are said to have valued the healing powers of the warm mineral waters. There are many tales of one old grizzly who came to the springs each night to cure a lame leg. He is said to have hung on to a branch with his forepaws, while dipping his aching leg in the refreshing waters.

North of King City is Pinnacles National Monument. Volcanoes raised mountains out of the earth at this point; then over the years the elements have cut and chiseled these into miles of rugged and interesting formations.

At one of the most unique stops along the coast, visitors may now marvel at what once was the unrivaled private estate of publisher

William Randolph Hearst. The wealthy man spent much of his lifetime, and about thirty million dollars, in creating his "Enchanted Hill"—the estate called San Simeon. From all over the world he brought the finest in furnishings and art. So many crates of irreplaceable objects poured in that some were never opened during Mr. Hearst's lifetime. The Hearst family has donated this estate to California, and it is now a state historical monument, where visitors can enjoy the fairy tale atmosphere of the place.

To the north, at Big Sur, many artists have gathered, building their picturesque houses and forming a well-known artists' colony. This point was the site of many noted shipwrecks until the famous lighthouse was built. When the light began to operate, one old native complained bitterly that it wasn't doing its job. He thought it was supposed to keep the heavy fog from rolling in.

During most of California's years under Spanish and Mexican rule, Monterey was the capital. The old custom house there is the oldest building in the state. A state historical monument marks the spot where Commodore Sloat first raised the United States flag over California. Another state historical monument at Monterey is the Robert Louis Stevenson house.

A famous scenic toll road, "Seventeen Mile Drive," takes visitors past Seal Rock, Cypress Point, and Pebble Beach Golf Course.

At Point Lobos Reserve State Park, visitors are intrigued by the sea lion rocks and bird island offshore.

The area is now the last stand for the noted Monterey cypress trees. Robert Louis Stevenson called these "ghosts fleeing before the wind." Their contorted branches and strange poses have been favorites of artists and photographers through the years.

One of the loveliest spots on the Pacific coast, Carmel, has been a favorite home of artists and writers since 1904.

This town tries to keep itself unique by banning street lights, neon signs, billboards, bowling alleys, trailer camps, used car lots, mortuaries, mail deliveries, and sidewalks, except downtown.

First preserve set aside by the state to save the great redwood trees was Big Basin Redwoods State Park, 23 miles (about 37 kilometers) northwest of Santa Cruz.

WHERE AN "EMPEROR" RULED

Few cities have so many strong admirers as San Francisco. The city has long been known as one of the world's most cosmopolitan. Much of the present city rests on man-made land, where the smaller hills have been leveled, and swampy or valley land filled in.

The bay, one of the most nearly perfect natural harbors on earth, is considered by many to be as beautiful as that of Naples. The San Francisco Bay is the largest landlocked harbor in the world, but strangely enough it was not discovered until 1769. Natural conditions hid it from seaborne explorers, who, for almost two hundred years, desperately looked for just such a harbor along a mostly unbroken coastline.

The city was not even begun until 1776, when the much older cities on the Atlantic Coast were declaring their independence from Britain. Until the gold rush, the little settlement slumbered, known by the mellow name of Yerba Buena. Captain John B. Montgomery captured Yerba Buena for the Americans in 1846. In 1847 the name was changed to San Francisco.

A cable car in San Francisco.

Surviving gold rush and crime and wickedness, gangsters and vigilantes, fires and earthquakes, the city today boasts one of the country's most mixed populations, with almost every race, nationality, and background represented.

The biggest cultural group is the Chinese, San Francisco is said to have the largest Oriental population of any city outside of Asia.

A Scot named Hallidie, who manufactured special cables for mining, wondered why his cables could not be made to haul passenger cars up the steep hills. People called the plan Hallidie's Folly, and the doubters gathered on Kearny Street one August afternoon in 1873 to jeer at the first test of the new-fangled conveyance, but they remained to cheer as the first cable car in history climbed pluckily up Clay Street to the top of Nob Hill.

Traffic pioneer of another kind and another day was Joseph B. Strauss, who built the Golden Gate Bridge. He was only five feet tall but a giant among bridge builders. Strauss' twenty years of planning and persuading and building came to triumph when on May 27, 1937, the bridge opened and there was a mad rush to be first. Many people claimed bridge titles, such as the first person to push a baby carriage across, or the first to walk across on stilts.

The San Francisco area's other great bridge, the Oakland Bay, was opened in 1936, and in its time was the longest bridge in the world.

San Franciscans have transformed a once-dreary wasteland into one of the world's most beautiful parks. Golden Gate Park forms a four-mile woodland retreat cutting from the heart of the city to the Pacific. It owes its development to master botanist John McLaren, who was still in charge while in his nineties. Within the park are an arboretum, zoo, museum, academy of science, Spreckels Lake (for model sailboats), and Kezar Stadium, home of the San Francisco Forty-Niners professional football team.

Another San Francisco stadium is Candlestick Park, eleven-million-dollar home of the San Francisco Giants baseball team.

Heart of the city is its seven-block cluster of buildings known as the Civic Center.

Towering over the center is the dome of city hall, with a design similar to the national Capitol but with a dome several feet higher.

San Francisco was among the first American communities to try a consolidated government for both the city and the county. This began in 1856 and has been a model for similar efforts elsewhere.

Federal and state buildings, public library, museum of art, civic auditorium, and opera house war memorial all occupy the Civic Center.

The historic opera building housed the Japanese Peace Treaty Conference in 1951. Earlier it had been the scene of the founding of the United Nations organization.

Famous names in San Francisco history and sightseeing also include Fisherman's Wharf, Mission Dolores, the Embarcadero, Telegraph Hill, Presidio, Seal Rocks, and Livestock Pavilion (known as the Cow Palace). This site of Presidential conventions seats 12,000 and is claimed to be the largest building anywhere without any pillars or obstructions to mar the view.

The city where Captain Fremont was so taken with a sunset view that he introduced the name Golden Gate to the world can boast of many advantages. Not the least of these is the fact that it consistently has the greatest income per person of all the major cities of the United States.

Oakland was once part of the 48,000-acre (about 19,400 hectares) Rancho San Antonio, owned by Luis Maria Peralta. The town was founded in 1851 by Horace W. Carpenter, who named it in honor of the evergreen oaks which were so plentiful. Lake Merritt is a 160-acre (about 64 hectares) lake entirely within the city limits of Oakland, and it includes a Federal refuge for birds.

Sharing Oakland Bay with the city of Oakland, is Alameda, site of the Naval Air Station.

Berkeley was also part of the vast Rancho San Antonio. The city takes its name from that of an Irish philosopher. The largest of the ten campuses of the University of California is the one at Berkeley, where the university began.

To the east of Berkeley and Oakland is Mt. Diablo State Park. A road spirals to the top of this 3,849 foot (about 1,170 meters) peak, the highest in the Bay region. A magnificent view of the area opens up for 200 miles (about 321 kilometers).

The Oakland Bay Bridge leading into San Francisco.

Palo Alto means tall tree in Spanish. It takes its name from the towering redwood which marked the spot, as a landmark for the Spaniards. The original tree is still standing. Other famous trees of Palo Alto are the sixty varieties that line a single street—Hamilton Avenue.

At San Jose is the strange Mystery House built by Sarah M. Winchester, widow of the Winchester Arms founder. Mrs. Winchester was told by a spiritualist that she would never die as long as she kept building her house. For thirty-eight years the sounds of carpenters, masons, and plumbers were never absent on a week day, as the wealthy eccentric poured her fortune into a fantastic sprawl of a structure which began to look more like a small city than a house.

Also at San Jose is the Oriental Museum, one of the largest collections from Egypt and the Orient in the United States. Besides the museum is the Egyptian Temple, reproduced to look like one of those that may have stood in the hot Sahara wastes.

Alum Rock Park near San Jose is known as Little Yosemite because of its rock formations.

NEAR NORTH

Only 27 miles (about 43 kilometers) north of San Francisco is one of the favorite natural spots of city residents—Mt. Tamalpais State Park. After climbing a twisting road almost to the summit, visitors have a spectacular view. They also enjoy the natural amphitheater called the Mountain Theater.

Another favorite recreation spot is Point Reyes National Seashore at Inverness. This area, unique in the world because of its mighty redwoods, has preserved many of the wonderful redwood forests. In Humboldt Redwoods State Park a portion of the road is called Avenue of the Giants. In this park is the Founders' Tree, honoring those who helped to preserve the redwoods; it is over 360 feet (about 110 meters) high and is considered the world's tallest tree.

Muir Woods National Monument is the only Federal Government preserve of virgin redwoods. This wonderful natural resource was donated to the people of the country by Congressman and Mrs. William Kent in honor of Muir, the naturalist, who did so much to persuade the people of California and the United States to save their natural wonders. Foot traffic in Muir Woods is so heavy that the great trees are threatened because of damage to their roots.

Richardson Grove State Park, north of Leggett, is another redwood preserve.

On the slopes of Mt. St. Helena in the Coast Range near Santa Rosa, the beloved English writer, Robert Louis Stevenson, spent his honeymoon. It was here he wrote his "The Silverado Squatters." The monument to Stevenson on the site of his bunkhouse near the summit is a statue of the author, holding an open book.

At Calistoga, the Mormon pioneer, Samuel Brannan, established a new spa in 1859, where people could take advantage of the natural mineral springs and mineral mud baths. He combined parts of the name of the Eastern spa, Saratoga, and the name of California to arrive at the name Calistoga.

In 1919 one of the finest of all petrified forests was discovered near Calistoga. Trees up to 126 feet (about 38 meters) have been found, with their details well preserved.

San Rafael was once the boxing center of the world. Many prominent boxers, including James J. Corbett and Battling Nelson, trained there. The San Rafael Civic Center was designed by architect Frank Lloyd Wright; it was one of the last of his major projects.

THE GREATEST VALLEY

To the east lies California's great central valley, with the capital of the state at Sacramento almost in its heart.

The seat of government in California has been at San Jose, Vallejo, and even Benicia. The old State House at Benicia, constructed in 1852, is the only original California Capitol building still standing that is older than the present Capitol at Sacramento.

The old Benicia Capitol has been restored, and in 1958 the Legislature met there again for one day to re-dedicate the building as a memorial.

However, Sacramento has been the capital city of California since 1854. Ground was broken for the present Capitol building in 1860. Fourteen years later, in 1874, the Capitol was completed. At the top of the dome on this classical building is a cupola supported by twelve columns. Its gold-leafed roof is crowned with a ball 30 inches (about 76 centimeters) in diameter. This ball is plated with gold coins, the symbol of California. An annex was completed in 1952 to provide much-needed additional room.

The grounds of the Capitol are among the most interesting and beautiful in the United States. Before the Capitol was completed, 800 trees and shrubs were brought in from all parts of the world. The effort has been continued to make the Capitol park a showplace of the world's trees, shrubs, and flowers, with more than 800 varieties now represented.

Sacramento remembers its founder, John Sutter, in many ways. Sutter's Fort and Indian Museum are a state historical monument.

Today, the city claims more autos per person than any other in the world. It calls itself the missile development center of the nation and camellia capital of the world.

Fresno and Stockton are other important central valley cities. Stockton is a prominent inland port. Early miners settled here and found more wealth in agriculture than they had discovered in gold. Fresno is noted for its annual Christmas Tree Lane, miles of beautiful cedar trees colorfully decorated for Christmas.

GOLD! GOLD! GOLD!

Reminders of California's great rush for golden wealth turn up everywhere in the old mining areas of Sacramento.

Columbia Historic State Park, near Sonora, has restored the gold town of Columbia.

Marshall Gold Discovery State Park's museum tells the story of the discovery of gold, and visitors may see the cabin and grave of the unfortunate discoverer, James Marshall.

In Mariposa, the Historical Center of the Mariposa County Historical Society re-creates the history of the area, with a typical street, stores, old school, assay office, saloon, gaming hall, and general store. Mariposa County Court House is the oldest in the state. It cost $9,000 to build, and the marks of the builders' planes and hand-blown glass can still be seen.

Placerville was once called Hangtown because of the number of hangings there. It rivaled San Francisco at one time, and was the home of such nationally famous men as Mark Hopkins, Philip D. Armour, and John Studebaker.

The state Capitol in Sacramento.

In 1856 Oroville became the fifth largest community in the state, after beginning only six years before as a tent city. When the Chinese came there in large numbers in the 1870s to work the gold, Oroville had California's largest Chinese population. Its Chinese temple is the largest authentic structure of its kind in California. Now only a small Chinese settlement remains there.

The Oroville Dam is an important part of the California Water Plan.

A NORTHERN PARADISE

Redwood Highway, U.S. 101, cuts north through redwood country for almost 300 miles (about 480 kilometers), for much of the way a four lane highway. As far north as the Del Norte Coast State Park, near Crescent City, the redwood trees start almost at the surf and grow up the steep slope. Here, also, rhododendron plants blanket the area and cover the ground with bloom during May and June.

Fort Ross State Historical Monument retains its memories of the only Russian settlement in the United States outside of Alaska. State Highway 1 runs past the partially restored stockade of Fort Ross.

Redding is the gateway to beautiful Mt. Shasta, 14,161 feet (about 4,300 meters) high. Shasta Dam, Shasta Lake, Burney Falls, and the old gold town of Shasta are other attractions of the area. Many of the original buildings are well preserved.

Not far from Redding, also, is Lassen Volcanic National Park. This volcano was active as recently as 1917. Boiling mud pots, boiling pools, and hissing steam vents can be seen.

Another area preserved by the Federal government for its volcanic interest is Lava Beds National Monument in the far north of California. This is a region of fantastic lava formations, of caves and of vent holes in the lava, some large enough to crawl through for a hundred feet (about 30 meters).

To the west is the salmon country of California. On the Klamath River, in some seasons, boats of fishermen have been so thick it could be possible to walk across the river from boat to boat.

86

A GRANITE FENCE ALONG THE BORDER

Stretching for a large part of the length of the Golden State along its eastern side is one of the most dramatic of mountain ranges, the Sierra Nevada.

Toward the center of the range lies one of the most breathtaking of all America's natural wonders. In 1851 Major James D. Savage went to visit the Yo Semite Indians. When he came within view of their home land, he thought it was the most wonderful sight he had ever seen; as far as can be told Major Savage was the first white man to view the "valley incomparable" of the Yo Semites, which, of course, has become Yosemite National Park of today.

Farther south, Sequoia and Kings Canyon National Parks are unlike any other area in the world. Although the sequoias are not so tall as their relatives the coast redwoods, they are much more bulky. The General Sherman Tree is considered the largest living thing. Its 3,500 year old trunk is 101.6 feet (about 30 meters) in circumference, the greatest in a forest of giants. The General Grant Tree, almost as large, was set aside by act of Congress as a living memorial to all the war dead of the nation.

Yosemite National Park

Emerald Bay, a section of Lake Tahoe

Hale Tharp discovered the Giant Forest when he went with his Indian friends to see a place where they walked in silence because of their awe for this spot. Present-day visitors experience the same feeling.

For thirty years, Tharp lived in one of the most unusual homes in history — a log cabin made of only one log! He put a window and door on one end of a huge fallen sequoia, hollowed it out and lived comfortably in what John Muir called "a noble den." This noble den is still to be seen as one of the attractions of the region, and because of the durability of the wood it will probably last longer than a stone castle.

Near Bishop, about halfway between Yosemite and Sequoia parks, another unique California natural wonder thrusts itself into the sky. This is Devil's Postpile National Monument. It looks as if some giant had piled at an angle thousands of huge carefully carved pillars, 60 feet (about 18 meters) long, like a stack of enormous posts. Nearby is attractive Rainbow Falls.

North of Yosemite, Donner Pass, through which the Donner party crept in tragedy, was for years the main overland route into California.

At Truckee the first California ski club was organized in 1913.

California and Nevada share another American beauty of the Sierra, Lake Tahoe.

Handy Reference Section

Instant Facts

Became the 31st state, September 9, 1850
Nickname—The Golden State
Full name—State of California
State Motto—*Eureka,* "I have found it!"
Capital—Sacramento
State flower—Golden Poppy
State bird—California Valley quail
State fish—California Golden trout
State stone—Serpentine
State animal—California grizzly bear
State song—"I Love You, California"
Area—158,693 square miles (411,013 square kilometers)
Rank in area—3rd
Greatest length (north to south)—770 miles (1,239 kilometers)
Greatest width (east to west)—360 miles (579 kilometers)
Coastline—840 miles (1,352 kilometers)
Shoreline—3,427 miles (5,514 kilometers)
Geographic center—35 miles (56 kilometers) east of Madera
Highest point—14,494 feet (4,418 meters), Mt. Whitney
Lowest point—282 feet (86 meters) below sea level, Death Valley
Mean elavation—2,900 feet (884 meters)
Number of counties—58
Population—22,611,000 (1978 estimate)
Rank in population—1st
Population density—127.6 persons per square mile (49 persons per square
            kilometer)
Rank in population density—14th
Population center—Kern County, 27.15 miles (43 kilometers) northwest
            of Bakersfield
Principal cities—Los Angeles   2,809,596
            San Francisco   715,694
            San Diego   697,027
            San Jose   770,527
            Oakland   361,561
            Long Beach   358,633
            Sacramento   257,105

You Have a Date with History

1540—Hernando de Alcarcón first white man to set foot in Alta California
1542—Juan Cabrillo explores coast of California
1579—Sir Francis Drake claims California for England
1584—Francisco Gali explores coast
1769—Father Junipero Serra and Gaspar de Portolá arrive in California
1770—Monterey founded
1775—First white child born in California
1776—San Francisco founded
1781—Los Angeles founded
1812—Fort Ross is built by Russians
1818—Hippolyte de Bouchard "captures" California
1823—Last of California missions, San Francisco Solano, established
1826—Mexico controls California
1827—First American, Jedediah Smith, comes overland to California
1839—John Sutter establishes New Helvetia
1846—California Republic constituted
1848—Treaty of Guadalupe Hidalgo, California becomes United States territory
1849—Gold Rush begins movement of population to California
1850—California becomes a state
1854—Sacramento becomes capital
1861—Telegraph lines come to California; war comes to United States
1869—Railroad crosses continent to California
1875—Bank of California closes
1879—New Constitution becomes effective
1906—San Francisco earthquake and fire
1912—Hiram Johnson runs for Vice-Presidency
1915—San Francisco and San Diego hold World's Fairs
1937—Opening of Golden Gate Bridge at San Francisco
1939—San Francisco launches Golden Gate International Exposition
1945—United Nations born in California at San Francisco
1948—Hale Telescope opens on Mount Palomar
1951—Japanese Peace Treaty conference, San Francisco
1955—First national political convention in California
1957—Big league baseball comes to California
1962—California claims largest population of any state
1963—Deep water channel opened to Sacramento
1970—Huge irrigation project ensured for southern California
1976—Ronald Reagan loses Republican Presidential nomination
1977—Drought and fires sweep the state

The Governors of California

Peter H. Burnett, 1849-1851
John McDougal, 1851-1852
John Bigler, 1852-1856
John Neely Johnson, 1856-1858
John B. Weller, 1858-1860
Milton S. Latham, 1860
John G. Downey, 1860-1862
Leland Stanford, 1862-1863
Frederick F. Law, 1863-1867
Henry H. Haight, 1867-1871
Newton Booth, 1871-1875
Romualdo Pacheco, 1875
William Irwin, 1875-1880
George C. Perkins, 1880-1883
George Stoneman, 1883-1887
Washington Bartlett, 1887
Robert W. Waterman, 1887-1891

Henry H. Markham, 1891-1895
James H. Budd, 1895-1899
Henry T. Gage, 1899-1903
George C. Pardee, 1903-1907
James N. Gillett, 1907-1911
Hiram W. Johnson, 1911-1917
William D. Stephens, 1917-1923
Friend William Richardson, 1923-1927
Clement C. Young, 1927-1931
James Rolph, Jr., 1931-1934
Frank F. Merriam, 1934-1939
Culbert L. Olson, 1939-1943
Earl Warren, 1943-1953
Goodwin J. Knight, 1953-1959
Edmund G. Brown, 1959-1967
Ronald Reagan, 1967-1975
Edmund G. Brown, Jr., 1975

Thinkers, Doers, Fighters

Luther Burbank
Juan Rodríguez Cabrillo
Kit Carson
Cesar Chavez
Charles Crocker
Cecil B. de Mille
Walt Disney
José Figueroa
John C. Frémont
William Randolph Hearst
Mark Hopkins
Collis P. Huntington
Helen Hunt Jackson
Hiram Johnson
Henry J. Kaiser
Jack London

Louis B. Mayer
John J. Montgomery
John Muir
Richard M. Nixon
Pío Pico
Gaspar de Portolá
Father Miguel José (Junípero) Serra
Chief Sequoyah
John D. Spreckels
Leland Stanford
John Steinbeck
Joseph B. Strauss
Levi Strauss
John Sutter
Eliza C. Tibbetts
Earl Warren

Index

94

95

PICTURE CREDITS

ABOUT THE AUTHOR

With the publication of his first book for school use when he was twenty, **Allan Carpenter** began a career as an author that has spanned more than 135 books. After teaching in the public schools of Des Moines, Mr. Carpenter began his career as an educational publisher at the age of twenty-one when he founded the magazine *Teachers Digest.* In the field of educational periodicals, he was responsible for many innovations. During his many years in publishing, he has perfected a highly organized approach to handling large volumes of factual material: after extensive traveling and having collected all possible materials, he systematically reviews and organizes everything. From his apartment high in Chicago's John Hancock Building, Allan recalls, "My collection and assimilation of materials on the states and countries began before the publication of my first book." Allan is the founder of Carpenter Publishing House and of Infordata International, Inc., publishers of *Issues in Education* and *Index to U. S. Government Periodicals.* When he is not writing or traveling, his principal avocation is music. He has been the principal bassist of many symphonies, and he managed the country's leading non-professional symphony for twenty-five years.